Managing Meetings

Paul Brown is a management consultant with an international practice. Trained as a clinical as well as an organizational psychologist, he is especially interested in how the private worlds of individuals fit the public worlds of business. He specializes in the management of conflict, senior executive development and selection.

Fiona Hackett graduated from the universities of Dublin and Belfast as an occupational psychologist, and spent three years in London working with Paul Brown. She is now a consultant with KPMG Stokes Kennedy Crowley in Dublin.

Bob Garratt is a management consultant, Chairman of Media Projects International and Visiting Fellow at the Management School of Imperial College, London. He is Chairman of the Association for Management Education and Development.

Other books in the Successful Manager series:

Paul Brown & Fiona Hackett

Managing Meetings

FONTANA/Collins

To H.M.R.C.,

who always asks the original question

First published in 1990 by Fontana Paperbacks
8 Grafton Street, London W1X 3LA

Copyright © Dr Paul Brown and Fiona Hackett 1990

Printed and bound in Great Britain by
William Collins Sons & Co. Ltd., Glasgow

—

Contents

Introduction

Could you, she said, *do something for us on meetings?*
Of course, we said.

It's a rule of good consulting never to say no until you know
what it is you are saying no to. So of course we said yes. And
then like all consulting that's worth doing it made us think again
about things we took for granted.

Then we wanted to write a book. Bob Garratt, the series
editor, said, '*Good idea*' – he often does, and it's very encouraging. Fontana said *yes*, and that was that.

One of us has spent more than thirty years enjoying meetings,
from University Rag and Union Committees to negotiating
salaries with the DHSS; from being part of the defence team in
hostile takeovers to delighting at that most skilled lawyer, the
late Paul Seighart. Invited to be a neutral chairman for a group
of potentially warring psychotherapists trying to resolve inter-
professional boundaries, he managed a complex process with
apparently unruffled ease. Such meetings are an endless source
of satisfaction.

The other is a determined non-joiner of everything. The
experience of committees is quite foreign but, to an occupational
psychologist, what the literature says about meetings is readily
accessible.

So from experience and some of what social and occupational
psychology have to say, we have distilled this practical guide.
Dedicated to the person who first posed the question, 'Do we
have to go on meeting like this?' we offer it to everyone in
organizations who wants to exercise skill in activities which

9

consume huge parts of their working (in post-prandial meetings, not always waking) time.

Many people perform so badly in meetings it is surprising they attend at all. Yet they are required to and do. The fact that meetings survive as the basic and main form of human encounter in organized society attests to their resilient nature and essential purposes.

Meetings are not an unnatural sport. On the contrary, they are attended by consenting adults. So basic are they to being human that their naturalness allows people to assume that there is no special skill attaching to them. Yet nothing could be less true. As in all common behaviour, from the most intimate to the most public to the most competitive, developing skill hones natural competence and makes the naturally less capable able to enjoy what they are doing.

The particular essence of skill is that energy flows productively in achieving a desired end. The greater the skill the more economically is energy employed or, conversely, the more effectively is a given amount of energy employed.

This book is about enjoyable economy of effort in the goal of making meetings more effective.

Have fun.

Paul Brown
Fiona Hackett
July 1989

1. What do we mean by meetings?

It is possible to have a meeting with yourself, by yourself, for yourself; but it is not easy. It usually requires contemplative isolation or the psychotherapist's couch. What we mean by meetings involves two or three or more gathered together for a named or unnamed purpose – which for a definition is about as vague as it is possible to get. Don't worry. We'll sharpen up on that, but stating it broadly reminds us of the essential quality of meetings. They are simply about people getting together for some purpose based upon talking rather than action.

The more people who come together, the more the meetings tend to have a structure – although in almost any profit-making organization huge amounts of time are wasted unprofitably through meetings whose purposes are ill-defined and whose structure is so loose it would fall apart if people weren't anchored to their chairs and could lean on tables and doodle.

A small hi-tech videodisc company had put a lot of time and effort into a series of meetings and presentations to a huge, recently privatized major utility. The small company was a new industry leader on quality and creativity. The major utility was grappling with its first serious commercial opposition. It was sharpening its product quality across the board and as part of that intention had (eventually) invited the small company to act as its consulting advisers in ensuring that the design and creativity standards of the video training and PR products it commissioned were to the highest standards the video industry could provide.

The video company went to a final pre-contract meeting with the utility people, and left three hours later exhausted and despondent. It wasn't that the contract wasn't going to proceed. It was that the meeting had been so badly prepared for, structured and run that they doubted whether they should commit their disciplined energies to clients who operated so far below their own expectations of efficiency. In the end they decided not to. It was the meeting that turned them away.

It was supposed to be a formal meeting, but it had no recognizable form, and it created no sense of intention of effective commercial outcome. Even its informality was a shambles. Mushroom farming or brewery parties seemed complex and subtle activities in comparison.

The distinction between formal and informal meetings is important – not, as is commonly supposed, because formal meetings have a person in the chair, someone taking minutes, and an organized agenda, whereas informal meetings often do not: but because exactly the same phenomena happen at informal as at formal meetings. At informal meetings people tend to forget that fact. So it is important to remind ourselves that the skills appropriate to formal meetings are equally applicable to informal meetings.

The phone rings on the desk. *Could you pop in for five minutes if you're free*, says the boss. Everything we say about the conduct of meetings applies as much to that five minutes as it does to the more formal boardroom in regard to what is going on, your part in it, and the outcome.

There is a second good reason for the distinction between formal and informal: because formal meetings have a much clearer structure than informal meetings it is easier to see what is (supposed to be) happening. 'Supposed to be' indicates that very often the formal variety fail in a number of ways, so we shall look at them first.

Before we do, some pointers about the book. We want it to make you think about, practise and enjoy skills by understanding what's really going on, not just what's supposed to be happening.

In consequence we have structured it so that the broad terrain is first established; some of the hazards are then explored; then practical action is detailed; the self-regulating questions and guidelines .essential to acquiring, maintaining and developing skill complete the order of our design.

So let's get on to the terrain of **formal** meetings.

They have three special characteristics:

1. An agenda
2. A person in charge in the chair
3. Someone taking minutes

Depending on the level of formality, there may well be extensive procedural rules about its conduct contained in *standing orders*. Standing orders simply organize and order the conduct of the meeting. But that level of formality is not our interest here. (Suffice it to note that the extensive rules which can govern meetings derive directly from parliamentary procedure and have been product tested and refined since the barons forced King John into signing Magna Carta.) In some settings – such as Parliament or battling at the TUC Congress – they may be crucial. In everyday commercial life they will rarely be invoked unless the going gets very tough and very political at board level, or in Annual or Extraordinary or Special General Meetings, where the conduct of the meeting itself may have legal ramifications. At those levels it is as important to know the rules, ruses and stratagems the laws allow as it is if you sit down with a chess grand master and try to take your opponent's queen. But we make the point in order to ignore it from now on, except in the chapter on being in the chair (chapter 8).

We are also not especially interested in the *minutes* of meetings, important though they are so far as the output of the meeting is concerned, as a record of what went on, and legally. But, since the form of minutes is often as indicative of an organization as their content is important as a record, we will dwell on them for a few pages. We have seen minutes which are almost a verbatim narrative of over several hours' discussion – pages and pages of them.

The trustees of a charity concerned with homeless animals had managed to merge their interests with another well-endowed but moribund charity whose objects and purposes were essentially the same. Having come into a good deal of additional money, the trustees began to differ about their aims: should they found and establish a new residential centre with the new funds or should they be used for developing the buildings and facilities of the existing establishment. Both were proper uses for the capital funds, and both were equally worthy. But the differences of opinion between those trustees who were minded to expand and those minded to improve were substantial, with neither side ready to yield.

The chairman was a fair-minded man, who through many years of charitable commitment and often hard financial times had prided himself on the support of his fellow trustees. As meetings became more and more contentious, he requested his secretary (not a trustee) to make increasingly detailed minutes. The consequence was that at each subsequent meeting the accuracy of her minutes was questioned, and endless minor amendments of nuance were made. Every meeting got off to a bad start as members limbered up for the real issue. Minor battles were won and lost, with an increasingly stressed chairman made miserable by the collapse of his major interest into warring factions.

The unspoken issue was in fact about who was to succeed the chairman, then in his late sixties, when his retirement became due. One trustee, an expansionist, particularly wanted the job. Two others disliked his manner and doubted his ability. They took up the improvement position. The overall aims and objectives (strategy) of the committee became lost in six months' fighting about unspoken issues. Hidden agendas are powerful things. *In due course the chairman, in his fair-mindedness, decided his only course was to stand down – a sad ending to his voluntary activities. The improvement lobby resigned in sympathy, leaving the expansionists to carry the day.*

While the squabbling had been going on, there had been a sharp surge in property prices. The charity could no longer afford to buy and renovate the property which the expansionist lobby had found. Nevertheless, they decided to buy it and try to raise funds to develop it – perhaps a reckless position for trustees to take. A year later, the property was still empty, and all funds raised were being devoted to urgent improvements at the original centre, threatened with closure by the local health inspectors. None of the trustees was enjoying their work. The minutes were still verbatim and occupying much time and energy.

So: one way of getting a feel of how well an organization is working is to see its minutes and ask: *Why does it do them this way?* Almost without exception a thoughtful answer will tell you a good deal about the behaviour of the organization in question.

The extreme opposite to the animal shelter episode is the company which produces its minutes in three columns. The first carries no more than ten typed spaces. The second covers half the page. The third is like the first. In the first column are the reference numbers of the items on the agendas, which throughout a financial year are numbered in accumulating sequence with a year reference. In the same column, and immediately underneath the item number, are those items relevant from the agendas for that year and the last relevant item for the previous year. In the main central column are the agenda headings underlined, and the decisions regarding each item. No discussion is recorded. In the right-hand column are the initials of the person required or authorized to take action. The first main item on subsequent agendas is to check action from the previous minutes. For meetings as long as those of the trustees, the minutes rarely cover more than two sides of A4 paper.

Minutes can have a style and a communicating life of their

own. The overriding principle is to keep them as brief as is consistent with accuracy about the outcome of each item. Sometimes a narrative form, sometimes a prescriptive, bullet-point form, is appropriate.

All that was rather by way of diversion. Perhaps we should explain why we find meetings so fascinating. The behaviour they produce and the underlying reasons are as exciting and dramatic as anything that happens in the world. The level of understanding you can develop and the skills you employ can make it so for you.

In very formal meetings the *agenda* may be precisely specified. At the Annual General Meeting of a public company the business to be completed is precisely defined in the Companies' Acts. Although there is technically an opportunity for shareholders to discuss matters and vote on whether to accept the accounts, elect directors and appoint auditors, the formality of the agenda and the rules which govern shareholders' power make it extremely difficult to do anything other than concur with the formal motions circulated in printed form prior to the meeting. Indeed it may all be over in two minutes. Yet without that two minutes when dissension and contrary votes could in principle occur (and very occasionally do), legitimate authority for the company to proceed on its commercial way would not be there. This kind of formality is a particular expression of the rule of law in a democratic country.

But generally it is informal meetings which are the familiar currency of organizational life. Every discussion of every kind is a meeting with an agenda, a chairman (someone who initiated it/ was in charge) and an outcome. A fleeting 'Hello!' passing in a corridor can carry an infinity of meaning and purpose. Equally the lack of encounter with someone can carry a wealth of meaning. Office politics, good and bad, are entirely about agendas – private and public. 'Reading', understanding and operating them is the stuff of everyday life. How well you can agree them defines your effectiveness.

The entrepreneurial and powerful boss of a construction company, self-made and getting on in years, had developed a substantial organization, but what gave him most feeling of power was not the resources he could command or the executives he could hire or fire, but making the major deals. He had made his fortune by buying land post-war, before building controls were eased, had done well out of subsequent property booms and become a survivor during property crashes. The marketplace acknowledged that he spotted the big ones ahead of the game.

In all major negotiations he had the chief executive of his operating companies take the chair in the group headquarters' second-floor boardroom, to which there were three doors. One came from his secretary's office, through which everyone had to pass to get into the room; one led into the private dining room; the third led out to the cloakroom and fire-escape landing.

At crucial points in the negotiations he would break his silence by saying he was going for a walk, and would indicate to the decision-maker in the opposite team that he or she might care to join him. They would leave together by the third door.

Pausing briefly at the cloakroom, as if preparing for a walk, he would stop at the first-floor landing and offer the deal he had been working out while listening to the negotiations. Such was the conspiratorial nature of the discussion and his skill at pitching it right that he rarely failed to get what he proposed. The walk was abandoned and they returned rather unexpectedly to the boardroom, catching people off guard, with the boss now taking over the meeting. Announcing that he and his (by then) co-conspirator had seen a solution, he would outline it and ask both sides to sort out the final details. He then left with his opposite number to go to the private dining room.

This pattern was invariable and to those who experienced it more than once as well as to his own operating executive the backstairs deal was well known: 'Did you get on to the

> backstairs?' *defined whether a negotiating meeting had been
> successful.*
>
> *The way he had founded his wealth remained top of this
> man's personal operating agenda, no matter what the formal
> agenda said. He went for outcome not content.*

Which brings us to the role of *the person holding the chair*. That
is where the power lies. Whoever is in the chair begins with all
the advantages. How those advantages are used depends upon
the skill of the chairperson. How s/he can be supported or
undermined depends upon the skill of the players, be they
members of a formal committee, an *ad hoc* task group, a project
management team or a sports club fund-raising group. Chairing
is so important there is a whole chapter on it (chapter 8) and the
person who does it. The chairman, madam chairman, chairperson, or just chair is as important to a meeting as a skipper is
to a boat. The formalities at the beginning of an agenda
('Apologies for absence') are like casting off the mooring lines.
Approving the minutes of the last meeting is like a mental check
that everything is shipshape and in working order. The voyage
really gets under way with the first serious item, usually No. 3 on
the list. The voyage will be calmer or more stormy, and the crew
will have a smoother or rougher ride, depending on the skill of
the captain in steering his way.

Now we come to **informal** meetings, and there is only one thing
to remember. They are exactly the same as formal meetings
without the formality!

A crucial distinction is the difference between *form* and
content. Form is what appears to go on; content is what actually
goes on. So it's the content (or process) of informal meetings
which needs to be borne in mind, not just the form. Looking at
content, we see also that even the most informal meetings have
form: an agenda ('What's it for?' 'What on earth was that
about?'); a chairperson (the person who initiated it); and minutes
– a record of what happened, even if it's only a distant memory.

In merchant banks, members of the corporate finance department who work on matters of extreme commercial sensitivity are required, as a matter of practice, to keep a day book of all their business conversations and encounters, however informal, so that there is a record of whatever may impinge upon the business.

But what we are interested in is what really goes on in meetings. How do you read the messages beneath the words? How do you understand what is happening (the process) as well as the content (the subject under discussion)? The starting-point is to understand the agendas: declared and hidden. Let's move on to that.

2. Nobody admits they enjoy them; everyone attends them incessantly

Meetings are costly ways of spending time. Peter Honey, an occupational psychologist, suggests that people at management level in organizations spend at least 60 per cent of their time in meetings of one sort or another.

Next time you're in one, make a calculation of the hourly rate for everyone there on a rough estimate of their salary or fees. Reckon how much their joint time has cost the company; and perhaps ask yourself if you could responsibly have paid that much for that quality of discussion and decision.

If you really want to frighten a management accountant, add the unseen costs – room rental, costs of serving tea and coffee, lost opportunity costs – and make a grand total. If meetings are boring you and are not worthwhile, table an item called 'costs and benefits of meetings' for the next agenda. You might do yourself and the company some good. One day someone will start an audit consultancy to bring the cost of meetings into management focus; just as there are consultancies which work on the costs of utilities in organizations. Utilities are supposed to facilitate work, but can drain the company's financial life-blood if their use is not controlled.

Even if the meeting is for a club or voluntary organization, with no direct costs involved, there are all kinds of lost opportunity and social costs – bits of DIY not done; children whose mother/father wasn't there at bedtime; and so on. Meetings can be compulsive and destructive. (But it's difficult not to go to them.)

A measure of their compulsive nature came from a 1983 survey of nearly 500 management leaders in the US: 72 per cent of respondents said many meetings are a waste of time. Some 90

21

per cent attributed failure to lack of advance planning and organization, while 78 per cent said they received no training on how to conduct a meeting and 76 per cent claimed their company had no guidelines for this. Almost every other aspect of a company's activities is regulated by agreed policies and practices. Most meetings are devoid of such essential underpinnings.

So what's their purpose? Why are they attended incessantly?

It's the theme of this book that there are overt and covert reasons for them: declared agendas and hidden agendas. At best they are a device for sharing information, reaching decisions, building teams, and focusing energies. At worst they are battle-grounds for interpersonal conflict.

A corporate finance director in a merchant bank found himself preparing to chair a meeting between warring factions in a merger which the bank had not helped to finance. A poorly thought-through set of agreements in the initial document had created a tail-wags-dog result, quite other than the declared intentions of all parties at the outset but difficult to shift once the tail had begun to assert its newly-discovered power. The declared intention at the beginning of the meeting: 'We've got to find better ways of working together', was continually subverted by all kinds of private agendas, most of which came down to the unsaid 'I don't trust you now anyway.'

Try this for an imaginative way out!

A company chairman had clever colleagues on a management committee who could not/would not agree a key strategy document. At a meeting he called to try to resolve the deadlock, everyone was handed a helium-filled balloon on entering the boardroom. The chairman said as he sat down holding his balloon, 'I've only two things to say at the start. At least we're all doing the same thing for once. And remember where the hot air is.'

It's very difficult to gesticulate, doodle or get up and leave while holding a large balloon, and it demonstrates rebellion too obviously to be the first one to let go. This pushed the meeting into different and more light-hearted gear. The chairman got the agreement he wanted and a good deal of amused respect as well.

A meeting can be for anything: it's a structure of infinite flexibility and purpose. Which is why, from occasion to occasion, it's difficult to recognize what kind it is. So we have to try to understand what's actually going on as against what seems to be going on. This is the distinction between *process* and *content*. The more you 'read' process the more sense meetings will make. Compare them with music. There are an extraordinary number of forms music can take – from Gregorian chant to heavy-metal pop. And that's only in Western culture. If you can learn to read the process – in musical terms, not just to hear the rhythm but to understand the underlying harmony – it becomes a great deal easier to know what's going on and to evaluate the output.

Superficially, meetings are about the skills of seeking information, considering proposals, reconciling conflicting views, summarizing opinions and reaching agreement. These are underlying themes common to all cultures and organizations whatever their rule structure.

A British Institute of Management pamphlet entitled 'Meetings – Setting Objectives', starts by describing a set of functions:

1. **Seeking** out the thoughts, practices and experiences of members on a particular situation or subject: to get the facts – the opinions – the judgements.

2. Drawing **conclusions** from these facts, views and experiences and identifying alternative proposals.

3. **Evaluating** these alternative proposals.

4. Making a **decision** and defining its manner of implementation.

5. Considering the **results** of decisions previously taken.

As the BIM points out, how these functions are pursued depends upon flexibility of thought among those present; the ability of members to communicate with one another; and the expertise of the administration before, during and after the meetings. But these processes often themselves depend upon deeper processes. Flexibility of thought may be related to fatigue or feelings of rage with another member. The ability to communicate with one another may in part be dependent on the hierarchy of relationships among those present and how particular individuals respond to authority. And the administration may facilitate or sabotage a meeting in a variety of ways. Thus, meetings aren't just what they seem to be.

Fortune magazine reported some work of Cynthia Stohl, a professor of Communications at Perdue University. Early organizational behaviour theory taught that there were four phases that any group goes through on meeting for the first time – what in business-speak shorthand have been called forming, storming, norming and performing.

In the first stage, participants test one another out and establish their relative positions. In the second, they find a cause for conflict or disagreement, usually about the aims of the meeting. In the third, they agree on certain rules of behaviour in their work together. And in the fourth the group gets down to its real task, and that's when the fun starts!

Professor Stohl argues, however, that the group rarely goes through these stages in any organized sequence. Most typically the members of the group jump back and forth between them. Knowing where it is, what it's doing, and making the right contribution at the right time is like jumping on to a moving bus. Jump too soon or too late and the consequences can be fatal.

On a bus the roles of driver, conductor and passenger are well-defined, but in meetings we have to learn what the possible roles are. Peter Honey describes co-ordinators, challengers, doers, thinkers and supporters. Professor Joe Kelly, of Concordia University, Quebec, sees the process as essentially adversarial – a group of opposing viewpoints in a struggle to achieve dominance. To avoid the traumas of meetings he prefers to run them as dramas. In his book *Meetings, Meetings: How to manipulate them and make them more fun*, Winston Fletcher describes the essential skills ('The Seven Deadly Skills') as aggression, conciliation, enthusiasm, interrogation, patience, sulks and withdrawal. But these descriptions don't tell us very much about the conditions (in the meeting; in the person) which fit them for the role. Which takes us back to process: what is it that is going on?

We can too easily assume that the words a person says are all we need to address ourselves to: that the emotional tone of what is said can be ignored. In fact, nothing makes people quieter more quickly or, conversely, more garrulous, than when their emotions are ignored. What is important to them is what they feel, because it is essentially from feelings that behaviour – including what we say, verbal behaviour – comes. The feeling gives meaning to our words (cf. piano played with and without feeling).

Picking up these crucial signals is a key function of the non-logical side of the brain – the right side in most people. This deals with impressions, intuitions and the half-conscious processes which logical thought often blocks out. With this aspect functioning, a person will pick up the process cues. All kinds of emotions may block it out: fatigue, incipient flu, organizational conflict, or worry about a personal problem.

One of the phenomena that can happen when people are in too logical a mode, with the non-logical part of the brain switched off, is that they agree for the wrong reasons. This has been called 'groupthink', when discussion can increase the uniformity of judgements. There may be a feeling of being part of a team but people in such situations are passengers or spectators, not players. To bring those who are effectively non-participants into play requires openness to disagreements, which of course produce anxiety. But, like a kaleidoscope, patterns will form only because the pieces are different, not because they are all the same colour, size and shape. The pernicious tendency to want to establish agreement is often at the expense of individuality. Then real agreements are replaced by closet-like behaviour which makes everyone's presence a waste of time. Knowing participants and their interests ensures that they feel involved and are brought in appropriately. This simple device can unleash the creative aspects of a person's contribution.

Another good way of getting people loosened up is to have two minutes of brainstorming. Take a topic quite unconnected with the agenda – 'How many uses are there for a hard-boiled egg?', for example. It's like limbering up before the start of a race – the appropriate muscles are flexed. Brainstorming sessions aren't actually much use in themselves, because lots of undisciplined items never go anywhere. They are no more like a real meeting than jogging with a high springing step is like a real race, but the flow of ideas sets that non-logical side of the brain working. Which can't be bad.

Perhaps the best way of getting a meeting functioning is to have briefed people well beforehand: discussed what is of special interest to them on the agenda, sounded out their ideas, and helped them formulate what they are going to contribute. Although it takes time to do this, the sense of involvement, knowing one's views rather than just speaking off-the-cuff, and (for the chairperson) being able to call on one member of the meeting to round out views, may coalesce into something which provokes agreement, and is a potent way of making a meeting work.

'Provokes agreement' may sound a contradiction in terms. 'Provokes disagreement' sounds more likely. But agreement is a state which arises naturally out of the dynamic of the meeting, just as discord and disagreement may. Agreement is something which is arrived at by processes which can be both understood and skilfully managed. Briefing is a good way to this end.

Another way of ensuring that the meeting works well is to

manage the controls effectively. The less intervention there is from the chair, the more people have a chance to express themselves. However, the key task for the chairperson is to steer the discussion, so timing of intervention is extremely important. A good chairperson co-operates with the forces present without losing sight of where he or she is trying to go.

Starting meetings on time is a key aspect of effective control. If it's not on track at the start, it may have difficulty in getting on track later. Making sure there are no interruptions from phones or other distractions is important, so is ensuring that everyone knows why they and everyone else are there.

3. The cynical view

Meetings are supposed to have a purpose. But we know from bitter experience that they can be costly, time-consuming, delaying, habit-forming, inefficient and pointless. All these are features of meetings which Larry G. McDougle at Southern Illinois University has noted, while Norman B. Sigmand of the University of Southern California has described them as the most costly form of communication in any organization. Take half-a-dozen executives with an average salary of £25,000 p.a; put them around a table for two hours; calculate on there being 235 working days in a year and 8 working hours in each day. That meeting results in around £130.00 of directly attributable costs. Because no one keeps a 'meetings' budget across the company as a whole, no one is working out the cost/benefit equation.

No wonder it's possible to become cynical without quite being able to attribute cause. Good managers get cynical if they see hard-won money wasted, yet meetings can be a leaky bucket in terms of the energy resources they demand.

In contrast to the cynical view, Wainwright asserts that every meeting is unique and potentially creative (a comforting thought, he hopes, in the midst of interminable rambling).

There are many different kinds of meetings: co-ordinating; morale-building; risk-sharing; briefing; problem-solving; consulting; information exchange; policy-making; airing grievances and letting off steam; persuading people to a point of view; exploring issues; acting out hidden agendas. No wonder the cynic can flourish, given this list and the fact that any or all may appear at a particular meeting.

All the time at meetings *facts* are briefly stated and *judgements* made. Unfortunately, as Josephine Klein points out, the division of ideas into facts and judgements, though commonplace in logic, is not commonplace in people's minds or in their behaviour. Values underpin judgements, and for most of the time people do not make their values explicit; indeed they may not be fully aware of them. In consequence, what is a self-evident fact to one person is by no means an established truth to another. Thus the data upon which a meeting relies – commonly agreed facts – are extremely hard to establish because the individuals' perceptions of those facts differ. This is true, too, not only of what happens *in* the meeting but of the activities which precede it: planning, preparation, context or venue, and the sorting out of an agenda. All set the boundaries for what is or is not possible in the meeting. The degree to which these serve personal ends or real, task-focused organizational ends is as much a matter for manipulation as any other aspect of a meeting.

To take one of these by way of example, *context* or *venue* has always been recognized as being of immediate significance in setting the style or time and making an unspoken declaration about the meeting's intended outcome. Politicians know this: the question of who visits whom is clearly seen in the question 'Your office or mine?' Power is defined in part by territory.

One type of divorce is where the man has left his wife when she had absolutely no wish to be separated or divorced. Among the resultant difficulties is one which often concerns the woman's territory. She tries to make it a condition of future meetings, or when the ex-husband collects the children, that he does not enter the home which previously they jointly shared. She can manage her rage and anger in a 'civilized' fashion by keeping him at a formal distance. By letting him cross the threshold, she feels a confusion about wanting him back but not wanting to be hurt again, and so not wanting him back, which can only be expressed in a firm setting of manageable boundaries.

The same sort of process can be seen in companies. The stylized formality of union-management meetings is part of an elaborate ritual for dealing with conflict, often to the exclusion of the real purpose of the company's activities except as defined in traditional worker/boss mythology. Similarly, the formal and seemingly endless procedures developed over hundreds of years by the law courts have evolved as ways of dealing with disputes and conflicts which may otherwise be unmanageable. 'I'll see you in court then' is a commercial threat which acknowledges that no constructive agenda is possible between two warring partners, and only the formal procedures and agenda of the court will allow a set of rules to be applied to find some resolution or verdict.

The agenda of the court is explicit: the establishment of truth. However imperfect their means, the adversarial processes developed in English law serve that purpose as well as they can. Courts which have no organized adversarial procedure as we know it – as in the Soviet Union or China, for instance – have quite different cultural agendas for crime, guilt and punishment.

Yet at times the law can appear, in the formality of the legal processes to which it gives rise, to be no more than a device for making lawyers rich – the undeclared or hidden agenda. It is always the hidden agenda which creates cynicism: the belief that things are not really as they are said to be. This process – a disparity between things as they are and as they are said to be – is corrosive of the human spirit and the cause of cynicism. The fact that many people *are* cynical about meetings attests to the difficulty of keeping them real instead of phoney.

Winston Fletcher has a wide collection of cynical views (or realistic ones from a cynical position!) in his book *Meetings, Meetings*, which the *Sunday Times* noted as containing 'twenty-one different strategies for bringing meetings to a successful conclusion – the one you want.' He quotes the scientist Sir Samuel Cocker as saying: 'A committee is a cul-de-sac down which ideas are lured and then quietly strangled.' Or Richard Harkness, in the *New York Herald Tribune*, who said: 'What is a committee? A group of the unwilling, picked from the unfit, to do the unnecessary!' And one Herbert V. Proknow was credited with observing; 'The usefulness of a meeting is in inverse proportion to the numbers attending.'

Part of the difficulty in trying to be realistic about meetings is the difficulty of arranging them. A paper in the *British Medical Journal* in 1964 entitled 'On the Probability of a Meeting', looked at the likelihood of being able to get numbers of busy people together within various periods of time. Beyond four the possibility of getting them together quickly became so unlikely as to make the task not worth attempting. If something so inherently simple is at times so difficult to arrange, again there is cause for cynicism. Indeed, one law of meetings – the Hackett-Brown proposition – states that, as the difficulty of arranging it increases, so will the likelihood that the first meeting will result in further meetings. Meeting becomes the sole object of the exercise and purpose is quickly lost.

Coupled with the difficulty of arranging them is the fact that they are often uncomfortable places in which to find oneself. Personal experience suggests that it is more difficult to walk out of a meeting than out of almost any other social encounter. So many people feel trapped and forced to suffer. And that is before the conflicts which classically characterize meetings.

G. R. Wainwright observes six main causes of personal conflict:

- being prevented from achieving something important
- someone present who simply does not fit into the group
- absence of clear facts
- poor listening skills
- interpersonal relationship difficulties
- unpleasant conditions

Andrew Grove, president of Intel Corporation, reported in *Fortune* magazine how he had discovered that constructive confrontation could channel people's conflicts and aggressive energies to work for the organization. He views dealing with conflicts as being at the heart of managing business, and focuses his manager's skills on attacking the *problem* not the individual. Good though it sounds, in practice people can get heated and need time to cool off. For most of us it is difficult to separate our ideas and views from ourselves, and an attack on the one feels like an attack on the self. The cynic would wonder: why spend time in such uncomfortable circumstances?

Nevertheless, the conflict model as the basis for management meetings is supported by Professor Joe Kelly, in an article in *Personnel* in 1987. He observes:

> Video studies reveal that a top management meeting is more likely to be an adversarial proceeding – not necessarily an open clash of wills, but a group of opposing viewpoints in a struggle to achieve dominance . . . if you want to survive in this paradoxical environment, you must learn how the players interrelate, what notes they play, and what weapons they consider acceptable . . . For many managers, a meeting is psychological warfare waged at nerve-racking intensity.

Who needs it? the cynic might ask. Who indeed? The process is fraught with the possibility of failure: poor agendas, poor chairmanship, the wrong people there, interruptions and irrelevancies, and people's thoughts going round in circles – as Peter Honey has noted. Added to the causes of failure are practices common enough for the British Institute of Management to describe them as '. . . sad examples of unprofessional and inefficient attitudes'. These are

- inadequate formality
- substituting people from one meeting to another
- background papers not read
- minutes not an accurate record
- topics not properly planned or controlled
- the chair allows too rambling a discussion

Managing Meetings

Fraught as meetings are with the possibilities of fault, failure, and unbridled power games, what sensible person would spend time in them? The cynic gets into a Catch-22, however. What sensible person does *not* spend time in them?

This takes us to the hidden agenda, so we're into the psychological view.

4. The psychological view

As a perspective on meetings, this is likely to be the least familiar to you. It is, however, the core of this book – not surprisingly, perhaps, because we are both psychologists.

If psychology is the science of human behaviour, it's remarkable how little of it is about when so much behaviour is going on everywhere, all the time. Some human behaviour is too banal to be worthy of detailed observation, and some too complex to admit of adequate explanation. 'I thought psychology was just commonsense' is still a frequent riposte socially on the discovery that one is a psychologist. But like all infant sciences, psychology has to start somewhere.

One aspect of science is to establish central concepts or constructs which weld a variety of phenomena together and make it possible to generalize about particular events or circumstances. In this sense, psychology is at its beginning; although it has established important constructs and models about the human condition, it is often less than precise in particular circumstances, and as a predictive science it still has a long way to go.

This may be because it is stuck within the boundaries of the physical sciences. The central principle of these – classically physics and chemistry – is to establish cause/effect relationships which are replicable and can therefore be tested experimentally. The problem with human beings is that their reactions may vary substantially as a consequence of their interdependence with other people. Like mixing a new set of chemicals together in unspecified amounts, people coming together may show surprising combinant effects. In consequence, if you're going to improve your knowledge of and skill in meetings, choose a situation which is well known to you if you can: where, if you want to experiment, *you* create the changes in the situation. What we want to do here is set down some markers about the psychological background.

There are four essential elements in answering the question, 'Why do we have so many meetings?' Put as simply as possible, meetings are about

- avoiding loneliness
- structuring time
- pursuing hidden agendas
- pursuing real tasks

Everyone likes to believe that meetings are about the last of these, but there's only a one in four possibility that any meeting is about pursuing real tasks. The apparent pursuit of real tasks may be an excuse for any one or more of the first three. And because we're human we can all get caught up in them, believing that we're pursuing real tasks but actually pursuing only (real) psychological tasks.

Avoiding loneliness

If we become philosophical for a moment and ask the basic questions of existence, such as 'What are we really doing here?' – a question which with less profound implications may have occurred to you in meetings – one answer concerns the nature of man as a social animal and the unavoidable fact of time.

Man as a social animal abhors loneliness. Despite the fact that two Australians will manage to collide in an empty airport lounge, while two Englishmen can create an impenetrable sense of space and privacy around them in the most crowded tube train, the human condition makes human beings dependent on one another for their psychological wellbeing.

The long period of helplessness which the human infant has is evidence of and in its turn creates this dependency. In extreme conditions, such as wartorn Vietnam, a child of six or seven may manage some kind of independent survival. In the affluent West, independence is marked with all kinds of rituals that begin with going to the local shops by oneself; going alone to school; holidays organized by the school; and finally holidays independent of parental control and the freedom of being twenty-one, which was dramatically reduced to eighteen at the stroke of the legislative pen. The Western child may not become economically independent until about twenty-one to twenty-four, after an extended period of education, so that more than one-third of a lifetime may begin with various forms of dependent social interaction. The social structures and societies which human beings build around themselves are nothing more or less than a reflection of the essential fear of being alone. For an infant being alone means almost certain death. For a child or teenager it feels bad. As an adult, complete isolation is seen either as a rare holy state or as a clinical condition often requiring the intervention of authority in one form or another.

Put in this context, meetings are an essential activity of human beings and in consequence have *a natural life of their own*. People need meetings, as meetings need people. Not meeting people is wrong, as Flanders and Swann might have said.

In essentially simple societies, such as a small Italian hilltop town, where life is bounded largely by agricultural rhythms which have existed for centuries, there is time to meet, and to stand and stare. But in societies which seek to control time and use it efficiently as one of the inelastic variables of production, the need for meeting often paradoxically consumes more time than in settings where the fear of not meeting is less probable. Thus one view of meetings is that they stem from a basic human need to avoid loneliness and to have significance through being known by others. Office politics play a great deal on the sense of significance for those who do or do not attend particular meetings. People derive their organizational as well as their personal significance from where they do or do not meet. This is as true of the smallest village cricket club as it is of the most sophisticated office.

Structuring time

Coupled with avoiding loneliness is the fact that we have to manage time. The only absolute certainty of our lives is that we will die, and the timing of that is unknown to us. We therefore have some unknown but finite period to fill.

At its simplest, life is about filling the unknown allotted time. Whether it has more or less purpose or meaning depends in part upon the quality of the way we fill it and upon the quality of the human encounters – personal and business – that we have on the way. Simple though these ideas are, they have profound ramifications: if there is only filling time and the avoidance of loneliness at the heart of everything we do, it is clear that human activity which involves meeting people is an attempt to assuage the uneasiness which loneliness and unfilled time would produce. It is not surprising, then, that in organizations meetings can take on a life of their own.

Nor is it surprising that time may be hijacked for personal ends. As this is the antithesis of an organization's needs and goals, in whose service people employ their time, many organizations have invested large amounts of effort (time, money and energy) in trying to structure time. 'Time management' is the catch-all phrase for this effort, and a good deal of consulting and elaborate diary systems are marketed to this end. Meetings are part of this effort, but the risk is that meetings, being a necessary part of human behaviour, will be sabotaged for the common purpose of simply meeting (the next section describes a cluster of circumstances, under the general rubric of 'hidden agendas', in which meetings might be sabotaged).

So the psychological perspective leads us to understand that meetings are difficult things to manage well because, being so necessary, they are subject to a variety of forces which encourage them to exist for their own sake rather than for the tasks to which they are ostensibly devoted.

The issue of the hidden agenda makes this even more apparent.

Pursuing hidden agendas

Hidden agendas arise because people typically come to be less concerned about the skills they bring than their own (unstated) needs and personalities.

In perhaps no other area of human activity is so much time wasted by so many for so few direct rewards. *Because* so much time is spent in meetings, there must be some reward to the participants. We have proposed that two basic rewards – reducing loneliness and filling in time – are gained. In the hidden agendas all kinds of personal, individual rewards are up for grabs.

Wainwright calls the hidden agendas 'hidden objectives', and observes that, quite apart from the legitimate (real task) reasons for the meeting, a person may call or attend a meeting in order to

- impress others not invited to attend
- discredit a rival, especially if the rival is not present
- show superiority, perhaps through having a special report on the agenda
- work out his/her frustrations or problems on other people at the meeting
- gain promotion by turning in a performance which attracts the attention of superiors
- build an empire by having people reporting to her/him
- make life difficult for others, possibly by calling the meeting at an inconvenient time
- defend his/her 'territory' by making it seem more important

- make life easier for herself/himself, possibly by allocating tasks to others at the meeting
- ride a hobby-horse which appears elsewhere on the agenda

This list could be extended considerably; there are as many hidden agendas as there are individuals present with personal agendas.

Is this not an extraordinary state of affairs? It would be difficult to imagine any other area of public, organizational human activity so prone to the interference of private, idiosyncratic actions as are meetings. They are often the backcloth to the private need to express oneself – a skill best employed on stage or screen, but there disciplined by the techniques the medium requires.

Suppose, in another context, a group of soldiers going into battle were allowed to express their inclinations. Disorder and chaos would ensue. But such circumstances are not unknown. The roving bands of *condottieri*, the mercenaries of the Middle Ages, were known for it. Massacres by sophisticated and apparently highly-trained troops, as at My Lai in Vietnam, showed how fine is the line between discipline and chaos, as did the rampaging of guerrilla bands in Uganda after the fall of Idi Amin. Yet in the battlefield of the boardroom, a production manager's weekly session, an advertising agency's meeting with a dissatisfied client, or the manipulations involved in allocating resources within the commissioning departments of a television company, metaphysical rape and pillage can pass for acceptable behaviour. Swathes are cut through human energies honestly employed in organizational goals, by the incompetence of the control and command structures of meetings intended to channel and direct those energies.

What then is the real task of meetings?

Pursuing real tasks

The real goal of a meeting is to get everyone's software working in tune. Its success can be judged by the subsequent actions of the participants. If their behaviour follows directly from the decisions made or information shared, it can be judged successful. To the extent that individuals pursue their own tracks, or fail to follow through on promises made or actions undertaken, it can be judged unsuccessful.

The software idea arises like this. In trying to understand what is going on in other people, think of them at birth as a sophisticated piece of hardware, needing to be programmed; and life experience as the means by which that programming is achieved.

Two bases of data are written in. One is to do with what is thought; the other with what is felt. An in-built instruction in all human beings is that they will fundamentally follow their feelings rather than their thoughts, as in the end it is feelings (or, inversely, the absence of feelings) which give meaning to thoughts.

Seen in this light, meetings are a means of ensuring that common goals are established by common experiences (being at the meeting; taking part in the discussions and decisions). It is the process of this common experience which makes the meeting more or less effective. To the extent that private, personal programming interferes with or overrides the common process, the meeting is only a vehicle for that individual to reinforce her/his programming rather than modify in pursuit of common goals. An autocratic chairperson may, of course, select a committee whose members have a tendency to say 'yes' to someone autocratic. Nevertheless, the meeting can be counted a success if its members have agreed with the chairperson for good reason. If it proves to be only a vehicle for the person getting his/her own way and the others acquiescing, interlocking private or hidden agendas have taken over the proper process.

This situation can sometimes be observed when a private company is sliding into bankruptcy. The accountant knows it but has not established a custom of independent views with the owner. The remaining members of the board owe their positions

41

to the owner's preferential whims and, despite being directors, have not managed to find the voice of individual authority. Organizational and sometimes personal disaster results. Only the liquidator is able to pursue the real task of the company – to pay its preferential shareholders and creditors as fully as possible – when the hidden agenda ('I always have things my way') is out of the way.

The means by which everyone at a meeting shares a common outcome is at the centre of the skills in running it. We take next a practical view, and then move on to the skills.

5. The practical view

Despite complaints that meetings are a waste of time, there is no doubt that in many situations they are a useful way of achieving your objective. Here we offer some reasons why they are seen as useful, and give some ideas of what they can achieve. Meetings can be used for

- consulting other people, so that you can form a view of a situation. A meeting is a way of gathering the information you want as well as picking up information you were not aware existed, so that you can form an opinion. Consulting is probably the most efficient way of forming a view. Through discussion of an issue, information often comes to the surface which you would not have got by asking questions, because you might not have known the right question to ask.
- serving the process of democratic management. Meetings which involve the sharing of information, the 'chewing-over' of problems or issues, and the deciding of solutions aid the democratic process. As a result, people feel included and involved in the process, and policies or decisions which then get implemented are more generally acceptable. This democratic process serves an important purpose in organizations. Research shows that morale is higher in employees as a result, and if morale is higher people feel more satisfied (psychologically) and motivation is increased.

However, this purpose may be abused. Meetings can then become forums for 'democracy in disguise'. The 'decision-maker' discusses the issues with everyone present, listens to their points of view and then (after the meeting) goes ahead with what s/he had decided to do anyway. The meeting was called to give a semblance of democracy. It does (initially, at least) achieve all the benefits of having a true democratic style, but such a process can backfire. When participants realize that they are being manipulated like pawns and that their input is being noted and thrown in the rubbish bin, morale sinks. At this stage you often hear people say 'Oh no, not another meeting. They are such a waste of time!' And they are, in the long run.

Here are some more uses for meetings:

- creating a springboard for action. Often the best way to stimulate a group into action is to call a meeting as a prelude to getting things going. Take, for example, the police super-intendent who has a murder to solve. Getting his staff together creates the ideal springboard for action and puts the hunt in motion.

- to *legitimize* or *empower*: a view on something, even if you are in charge, often needs the support and agreement of colleagues. A perfect use of precious time is for the agenda to legitimize and empower your view so that the process can move forward. This need of support and agreement for implementation has some similarity with the democratic process.

- meetings save time. True, they can use a lot of time, but if run efficiently they save time. But there are those which are a total waste of time, like the chairman who called a meeting to tell the directors when he was going on holiday. A memo could have achieved just as much.

- people work in teams for many projects and in many situations. A team or group is inconceivable without meetings. Getting together at the beginning of a task or project is to share out the workload, decide what has to be done, the time-scale involved, and who is capable of doing what. This is most practically done by meeting with those involved and getting it sorted out.

- similarly, a well-run group or team meeting will mean that skills and resources are available at the highest standard. The knowledge base of a group is greater than that of one person, and the range of skills will increase when pooled.

Group research indicates that peole working in a group or meeting stimulate each other. A specific use of this theory is in the specialist meeting called 'brainstorming' (briefly touched on already). Brainstorming is used to come up with lots of ideas or solutions in a specified period of time. Discussion of the ideas does not take place at this stage; people simply stimulate one another through their ideas.

Meetings heighten everyone's awareness of other people's problems or points of view. Sharing and giving a point of view are crucial for better communication.

When meetings do not work

A practical view does not necessarily imply a positive view. Looking at meetings practically, one can say that many are a waste of time. Often the only outcome is increased conflict among members, or the time is used up on redundant or personal objectives. Take, for example, the situation where three or four heads of department come together to discuss how their budget spending is progressing. One member is annoyed with one of the others, and decides to use the meeting as a means of making the other members aware of this, and so the time is used on one person's personal objective.

Besides the positive aspects of communicating in groups, there is a negative side. This can produce group meetings where some do not state their views, fearing negative evaluations. Another phenomenon is what has become known as 'groupthink' (mentioned previously), where social norms accepted by the group take over to the detriment of the tasks facing them. It is *over-conformity* when people in a group become so inward-looking or cohesive that they come up with less than adequate answers, and is especially characteristic of people who know one another well and have been meeting regularly for a long time. One of the most quoted examples of this is what happened at the Bay of Pigs, when the American administration demonstrated perfect groupthink. I. L. Janis, an American writer who has described what he calls 'victims of groupthink' analysed the events and concluded that the group which deliberated on the Bay of Pigs decision included men of considerable talent:

> *Like the President, all the main advisers were shrewd thinkers, capable of objective, rational analysis, and accustomed to speaking their minds. But collectively they failed to detect the serious flaws in the invasion plans.*

There are general symptoms of groupthink which may be worth looking out for in a group you meet regularly. They may be easier to spot if you have just joined as an outsider. The group may be under the illusion that everything decided by the majority is a unanimous decision, and it emphasizes team play. They may have a view of the opposition as being inept, incompetent and incapable of countering any action by the group, no matter how risky the decision or how high the odds against their plan succeeding.

1. **Self-censorship:** group members avoid overt disagreements; faulty assumptions are not questioned and personal doubts are suppressed in favour of a fatal sense of group harmony.

2. **Collective rationalization** operates to comfort one another in order to discount warnings that an agreed plan is either not working or not likely to work.

3. **Self-appointed mindguards** operate to prevent anyone from undermining the group's apparent unanimity and to protect its members from unwelcome ideas.

4. **Pressurizing** a dissenting member directly or by implication.

5. **Self-righteousness** leads members to believe their actions are moral and ethical, thus inclining them to disregard objections to their behaviour.

6. **A shared feeling of unassailability,** marked by a high degree of *esprit de corps* and inordinate optimism which disposes members to take excessive risks.

Most people have experienced groupthink at one time or another, although it is not inherent in group decision-making activities and can be avoided. Here are some tips for preventing the appearance of groupthink:

1. **Leader encouragement:** encouraging subordinates to speak out, feeling free to disagree and to contribute the best of their thinking, is an important role of the group leader.

2. **Diversity:** structuring the group or sessions so that there are different viewpoints.

3. **New approaches and new people:** sometimes spending time thinking about something alone, or discussing it with an 'outsider' can result in refreshing perspectives.

4. **Taking time to examine group processes:** spend some time questioning: Who does the most/least talking? Why? Are all members participants? Who talks to whom? What is called a 'process consultant' may be useful here – a person trained to observe and feed the information back to the group so that it understands its characteristics and can adapt in consequence.

6. Skill in meetings

Meetings revolve around the agenda. The agenda is like a map on a journey, with each item being a hamlet, village, small town or large conurbation. Some only merit a glance, and are ticked off almost in passing. Others are worth stopping off at and enjoying. Others feel like a struggle, and there's a risk of getting jammed up. Trying to travel from the north-east side of Leicester to find the M1 on the south-west side is a nightmare of roads made into through traffic routes for which they were never designed. The relief at getting through is exactly the same as a difficult item on an agenda safely negotiated.

This chapter starts with the agenda, and then addresses the five key questions which underlie skill in meetings:

> *What is it for?*
> *What can I contribute?*
> *What do I want to get out of it?*
> *What should I do [have done] to prepare?*
> *What outcome tasks do I have to complete?*

Chapter 7 looks at the key functions which any committee or meeting member has, while chapter 8 considers the special skills of the chair. Chapter 9 ties it all together in proposing ways that you can practise becoming skilful at meetings, have fun, and make meetings work well.

Back then to the agenda. Leaving aside for the moment the question of the hidden agenda that we explored in chapter 4, there are two other forms of agenda of which it is important to be aware.

The first is what is commonly understood by the term agenda, in that it is an **explicit** set of statements on paper about the business of the meeting. A rather stiff but very thorough agenda for the Annual General Meeting of a professional association looked like this:

10TH ANNUAL GENERAL MEETING OF THE ASSOCIATION

Agenda
1. Apologies for absence
2. Minutes of the 9th AGM (circulated)
3. Report from Finance Committee (circulated)
    3.1 To receive the audited accounts for 1988/89
    3.2 To approve the accounts
4. Report from Professional Standards Committee (circulated)
    4.1 Discussion thereon
    4.2 To approve the report
5. Report from Training Committee (circulated)
    5.1 Discussion thereon
    5.2 To approve the report
6. Report from Journals Sub-committee (circulated)
    6.1 Discussion thereon
    6.2 Proposed increase in journal subscriptions
    6.3 To approve the report
    6.4 To approve the journal subscription for 1989–90
7. Matters arising from members (previously notified)
8. Chairman's overview of 1988/89
9. Any other business
10. Date, place and time of 1990 AGM
11. Concluding remarks

Arguably this might have been presented in a neater or more compressed form. Nevertheless, it is extremely clear what is to happen, and the point at which anything that might be of interest to those attending can appropriately be discussed.

Typically agendas start with apologies for absence, followed by confirmation of the minutes of the previous meeting, and end with Any Other Business (A.O.B.) and the date of the next meeting. To go back to the metaphor of the journey, it is rather like getting the car out of the garage, driving through familiar streets, and putting it away again at the end. Of course, squabbles may develop early on in a journey. The earlier example of how the animal charity spent more and more time on the minutiae of the previous minutes was exactly that squabbling rather than getting on with the journey. But in a well-organized setting, the preliminaries are readily dispensed with, and the main matters of the agenda addressed. On a journey, it is both the familiar and the new which attract; so in an agenda it is the surprises which add zest to the activity, while the main destination is kept well in mind.

Most meetings which have agendas do not happen in isolation. They happen in a context, and usually as part of a sequence. The sort of meeting with an explicit agenda which happens in context but only once is the sort of meeting called by a local planning authority – or perhaps more usually demanded by a local residents' association – to discuss, say, the consequences of a new housing development on a village where green belt land is being released.

The agenda may be stated on a public notice board or in the local paper, typically billed as a consultation exercise. It is a fertile ground for people to turn up with all kinds of hidden agendas, ranging from feeling personally aggrieved to the outright political. But at least the starting point was explicit, in exactly the same way as the association agenda previously described was explicit.

A very common form of meeting, however, is one in which the agenda is **implicit**. It's not necessarily that the person calling the meeting has any hidden motives, (though s/he may have), but that the agenda is clear in the mind of the person wanting the meeting but not in the mind(s) of those attending.

This implicit agenda is most typically seen in hierarchical organizations – the kind most people work in. Someone in a senior position says '*Drop in for a few minutes after lunch will you, Bob, and see if you can get Jane and Alan along too.*' Clearly it's for something, but Bob probably has almost no idea what. He arrives as de-skilled as it's possible to be. Which takes us to the first key question underlying skill in meetings:

What's it for?

This is a question that can be put in a variety of ways. Rather than say 'Right-o. Will do', Bob might more usefully have said: 'Right-o. Anything you want me to bring or prepare?' At least it makes his boss reflect for a moment on what he is calling the meeting for. A reply which says: 'No; don't bother, I'll tell you when you come' would leave him bereft of the prior thinking time of three colleagues. But anyone wanting a meeting is likely to fall into the error of believing that those who come can be brought up to speed quickly and efficiently, whereas the person who called the meeting might have had the matter in hand – on their own personal agenda – for a long time. Instead of making it explicit when involving other people, s/he keeps it implicit until the last possible moment.

Bob might have been more direct. '*Yes, of course, that's fine,*' he says in response to the request/implied instruction to be in his boss's office after lunch. '*What's it about? I'll do some thinking before I come and brief Jane and Alan.*' A lack of real response now could hardly be put down to lack of trying to find out.

Another way in which the implicit agenda occurs is when the person calling the meeting shares the worry not the problem. Take Bob and his boss again. Bob is manufacturing manager, his boss the production director. Phoning Bob, the PD says: '*Bob, I'm concerned about the raw material delivery times you sent up this morning. Look in and see me as soon as you can, will you*?' Although Bob knows where the area of concern is for his PD, has nothing definite to work on. The agenda as stated is the PD's concern, while the real agenda needs to be about action. Had his boss framed his invitation more directly in outcome terms, Bob could have been more sure how he might contribute. If the PD said: '*Bob, I'm concerned about the raw material delivery times you sent up this morning. Come and let's see what flexibility we can find in them,*' would set Bob's thoughts along specific tracks right away. The agenda has become explicit and the meeting is likely to start off with two people's minds already engaged. So the question 'What is it for?' suggests that people both calling and attending meetings need to have a rule: What's the way people's resources can be most productively devoted to the matter in hand?

What can I contribute?

That the answer is sometimes 'nothing' is worth bearing in mind. The bane of an efficient committee is to have people speak who have nothing to say. The only proper contribution may be to support what someone else has said and then shut up, rather than repeat it in a different form.

In a grand house in the Midlands a meeting had been called of people who might be interested, one way or another, in developing the local voluntary services for helping the recovery of alcoholics. Apart from the elderly titled owner of the house, who was acting as host and de facto *chairman, there were three managing directors from local industry; a magistrate; a psychiatrist; a general practitioner; and a senior police officer. Only the industrialists knew one another. One was on first-name terms with the chairman; he also knew the magistrate and appeared to have a nodding acquaintance with the police officer. The police officer and the magistrate appeared not to know each other. The chairman had at one time been on the local bench, but did not know the magistrate directly. The psychiatrist and the GP knew each other professionally but apparently not well. Present also was a representative from a national organization,*

53

whose concern was to see local initiatives got under way. The main item on the agenda was to consider how a local organization could be established.

Unfortunately, the chairman was substantially past his best. Whatever skills he might have had as a younger man were no longer evident, yet the group constantly deferred to his inconsequential remarks and anecdotal interruptions. Although the national representative had come prepared with a flip-chart and hand-outs, he was not very articulate and obviously felt ill-at-ease in the gathering. The industrialist who knew the chairman wanted to consider ways and means of raising money, to the exclusion of everything else. Those remaining spoke when spoken to or filled uneasy pauses unproductively. The psychiatrist, who ought to have had a great deal to contribute, was of a reflective nature, unwilling or unable to sell the needs of the local community and his patients to the group as a whole.

Despite a great deal of initial goodwill, the meeting ended without anything being decided, and was brought to a surprise conclusion when a dinner gong sounded and the chairman explained that in five minutes he had to entertain guests elsewhere. It took another year before a separate initiative on the same issue was taken, this time much more effectively.

The flaw in the setting up of the meeting had not been so much a failure to state the purpose, but the absence of the key question *at the appropriate time*. A key contribution ought to have been that one person made contact with all those attending before the meeting; had sounded them out and talked through the options, and had guided the meeting as one of those attending.

The meeting had in fact been arranged by the national representative, who had his well-known national chairman ask the local land-owner, an old friend, to make a series of telephone calls inviting those who came to attend. There had been no follow-up to these calls. Not only had a key contribution not been made prior to the meeting, but no one had sufficient clarity of purpose beyond the main broad question to be able to contribute effectively especially under the adverse conditions imposed by the context and the lack of chairmanship. In the end, a meeting can only be as good as its chairman. It may sometimes get somewhere despite its chairman, but never as far as with a good one (see chapter 8).

What do I want to get out of it?

This lies at the centre of the whole meeting process. It's the focus of the private, hidden agenda as well as the overt, public agenda. You must get something positive out, even if it is no more than your enjoyment of being there.

It is perfectly right and proper that what you want to get out of a meeting is what the organization – of which you are a part – wants. Its goals can be your goals, and in most circumstances will be. Your task is to facilitate the functioning of the meeting (see next chapter) in whatever ways that will help those attending arrive at, and be committed to, the goals you share with the organization.

It is also perfectly right and proper that you should consider your own goals, which may be complementary to the organization's goals or, in one form or another, in opposition to them. The meeting is, after all, a very special arena of interaction with your colleagues. The expectations they have of you, and you of them, will often be built up largely from common attendance at meetings.

Knowing clearly what the meeting is for and being clear what you can contribute to any particular item, will give you the freedom to consider what you might want to get out of it. What might your goals be?

In essence, they revolve around taking a political view of the context of your attendance: does it arise from your main source of employment and your investment in your career; or from your local village or town setting; or is it as a member of the new governing body, with increased powers, in your child's local school. Every meeting has *and should have* a personal context as well as a public one. If politics is usefully defined as the art of the possible, then most meetings are imbued with politics whether we like it or not. But the key issue is, should your personal agenda override the public agenda at any point?

Our advice would be, 'Never . . . well, hardly ever.' There is nothing more tedious to other members than to find that one person is so locked into personal issues that s/he is not contributing to the purpose of the common agenda. If personal issues are so pressing, deal with them on an agenda specifically (if only implicitly) set up for that purpose. It's rare that there are any brownie points to be had by hijacking anything. This is especially true of meetings: yet lack of skill can create unwitting hijacks, of which the noble chair of the meeting for setting up a voluntary alcoholics organization was a good example. Too many people were there who hadn't had a chance to get their private agendas out of the way, and in consequence little was gained.

Yet this boundary between the public and private – what is supposed to be going on as against what may actually be going on – is worth stressing. Many people make the mistake of believing that a meeting should be *either* about what it's supposed to be about *or*, if it's about private agendas, shouldn't be held at all. That would be one way of cutting down meetings, but is quite unrealistic. For the essence of all interpersonal encounters is that there will be all kinds of person-to-person (private) agendas going on: the messages underneath the words; the messages conveyed non-verbally by postures and positions. The issue, and the basis of skill, is in knowing that all meetings are about both the public and the private agendas, not either/or. Once you see this as the working basis, you will be free to decide at what level you choose to operate – the public, the private, or between the two. We would always recommend the latter, keeping the preponderance of your involvement firmly on the public, overt side. As we've said, there are only negative brownie points to be had by letting the personal take over the public.

One of the more irritating habits of politicians speaking in public is a tendency not to answer the question asked but the question they wanted asked. Nevertheless, the skilful politician deals initially with the question as put – the public agenda – and then converts it into his own statement – the private agenda. S/he gains much more credit by simply saying: 'I'm not going to answer that: let me tell you what I think people really want you to ask me', than by ignoring the question in a welter of verbiage. At least the public concern, rightly or wrongly surmised, has been addressed directly by the politician, who in consequence comes across as a direct individual rather than being concerned only to state his/her position, and listen to the sound of his/her voice.

In any well-functioning meeting or committee, the unstated rules say something like: 'We tackle the issues on the agenda in an organized way: everyone is free to contribute: the authority of the chair is obeyed: and we will pay proper regard to everyone's point of view in getting to conclusions as economically but as fully as we can.'

The chairperson is not so much a referee as captain of the ship. In the end her/his decisions affect the total direction. It makes no more sense to work with a poor chairman than to sail with an untrained skipper. Nor, taking the analogy further, should anyone be a member of a meeting unless s/he has got crewlike skills up to, and sometimes including, capability to take over the helm. A bit of course-correction, or pointing out an unforeseen hazard, is always welcomed by a good skipper when properly offered by a member of the crew; similarly in meetings. A well-prepared member may, for instance, see linkages between items which the chair did not foresee or could not have known. Brought skilfully forward at the right time, these make the passage of the meeting smoother.

So, in the question of the balance between personal and public agendas, there is no single answer, except that they be kept in proper relationship one to another. Both should be acknowledged as important.

What should I do (have done) to prepare?

This is more often honoured in the breach than in the observance. People come to meetings badly prepared and think on their feet: in consequence a good deal of time is wasted. One would not attend a dinner without giving thought and preparation to the occasion, so attending meetings requires proper preparation for being there.

This is a counsel of perfection, but worth aiming for. Many people arrive at meetings in the same frame of mind as sending out for a home-delivered pizza to entertain guests. The encounter with the people might be fun but little preparation has gone into it.

Preparation can begin only with a proper reading of the agenda and the minutes which back it. If it's an informal meeting, finding out what the agenda is – making it **explicit** rather than **implicit** (see Bob and his boss earlier) – is the best you can do. To read an agenda properly may take no more than five minutes, with two minutes given to each of the most important items and more time if any one item is your responsibility. Information circulated in advance is infinitely more valuable than that delivered off the cuff. A smooth-running committee should assume that documents circulated in advance have been read. It is neglectful not to have read these papers. Not to understand them, or to want to ask questions about them is quite understandable. But not to have read them is inexcusable. A new committee or meeting may have to note these ground rules. Only an effective chairperson can instil them, because s/he has the power to conduct the meeting on the assumption that documents have been read.

It is part of the same discipline to start a meeting on time. There are good and legitimate reasons why a person may be late for a meeting, but not many. The habit of being in time is part of proper preparation.

If there is an item which is your particular concern, and it requires some form of verbal or visual presentation, the rules that 3M Corporation developed are worth following. A visual should express only one idea, be no more than six lines long, and have no more than six words.

Additionally it should be

- easy to read with large, clearly defined letters and numbers
- neat and simple
- use high contrast definition

It is also a good practice to state the conclusion first – 'bottom-line it' straight away, so that people have the chance to become familiar with your point of view and assimilate it into their thinking as you talk. It may also give them longer to develop counter-arguments, but if it's counter-arguments that spring to mind they are more likely to be modified by what you say than if the counter-arguments come straight after your final statement of conclusions.

A meeting is best understood by the effectiveness of its outcome. Outcomes are a function of how individuals commit themselves to the agreements reached, and this brings us to our fifth question.

What outcome tasks do I have to complete?

A common phenomenon of voluntary meetings – the committees that proliferate in professional or academic organizations, for instance – is that individuals promise to complete some work for the next meeting and fail to do so, appearing with fulsome apologies and an implied promise to do better the next time.

A number of things are happening here. Either the person is a chronic non-completer, and is as much a menace on a committee as someone wearing slippery shoes on the deck of a boat. They're simply not reliable; or, more probably, the atmosphere and pressures of the meeting encouraged the person to comply with a request for action without having a similar motivation to complete the action.

A good chair will always ensure that anyone saying 'yes' to a task has a proper appreciation of the time, effort and importance of the task. *Pari passu*, the member of the committee has an obligation not to say 'yes' if s/he really means 'no'! Saying 'yes' in such circumstances means one has slipped into a private agenda (wanting to please: not wanting to seem awkward) which while appearing to relate to the public aspect of the agenda doesn't at all. There is also the person, often found on committees, who chronically takes on too much work. In consequence s/he really does mean to complete what was requested, but is running a private agenda of needing to feel hassled. They often do complete, but late, and this hinders the effectiveness of the committee.

In paid work situations, these phenomena are not so apparent, as there may be severe sanctions for failure to complete what is promised. More typical of these situations is the person who is playing the hassled game, and working out a private agenda ('poor me') in a public context where, paradoxically, s/he may get praise for being so busy and working so hard. Such a person tends not to enjoy their work and is often a prime candidate for a heart attack.

So, skill in meetings comes from five simple questions which lead to five equally simple rules. Setting all the rules together, they say:

1. It's the job of everyone involved to clarify at the earliest possible opportunity what the meeting is for.

2. The meeting will only be as good as the contribution I make.

3. A proper balance needs to be maintained between the public and any private agenda(s). Both are important, but there is severe risk in letting the private swamp the public.

4. I have an obligation to take time to read the agenda, assimilate any papers and distribute any material relevant to an item with which I am dealing.

5. I will do whatever I have promised to do arising from the meeting, and won't promise those things I can't realistically fulfil.

If these sound a little like scout and guide honour codes, so be it. Simple rules of behaviour often lead to surprisingly effective results.

7. Being yourself but being clever about it

From everything we have said so far it is clear that the view we take of meetings is an interactionist one. By that we mean that your interpersonal interplay with the others at a meeting affects them and the outcome. Similarly, what they do affects you and the outcome.

In organized team games such a view is axiomatic. An enormous amount of time, money, effort and skill is put into defining players' roles, positions and specific contributions. It *has* been known for a goalkeeper to run up the field and score, though it's rare. By and large, the players in a team know their roles and functions and develop their special skills.

In less structured but nevertheless interdependent activities the skill with which a person perceives what is happening and adapts to the situation is also apparent. But it is surprising that so little skill training is put into meetings. Someone is much more likely to be 'dropped in it' than helped out of a difficult situation. In complex circumstances where many people are not sure of their skills, or indeed what skills are required – and where additionally a wide variety of personal agendas may be operating – perhaps it's not surprising that people don't enjoy meetings and committees and see them as a chore rather than a source of satisfaction and pleasure in the exercise of a skill.

Josephine Klein is an early and good proponent of the interactionist position, and it is largely from her writing (*Working with Groups: the social psychology of discussion and decision*) that our views have taken root. In order to function effectively and make decisions, a group must, she observes, have the fullest possible *information*; on the basis of which *views* are expressed and *proposals* made; until finally *agreement* is reached among the majority of those present or a solution is imposed on the basis of the authority structure in the meeting.

As we have already seen, however, this process is often interrupted by the private agendas (what Klein calls the private preoccupations) of members.

Of course, self-expression may be appropriate as well as inappropriate. In general, self-expression, e.g. 'I like that idea' (it fits in with my ideas and value systems) is appropriate when it is in pursuit of the common objective. It doesn't always have to be supportive, and indeed the expression of disagreements in a discussion is a means of getting towards solutions. But when self-expression is manifestly redundant to the task and hinders rather than helps, clearly it is being done by someone who is either acting as a spoiler or who is simply unskilled.

The interactionist ideas are shown in this diagram:

1	2		3
Express positive/ supportive emotions	Relates directly to tasks		Express negative/ disjunctive emotions
SHOWS solidarity	GIVES	suggestions opinions	SHOWS antagonism
RELEASES tensions		information	CREATES tension
EXPRESSES agreement	REQUESTS	suggestions opinions information	EXPRESSES disagreement

This diagram defines the boundaries of the skills needed (Columns 1 and 2) and those not needed (Column 3). To teach the skills of column 3 would be like teaching people how to foul deliberately in team games. The skill to play also implies the skill to foul.

It may be helpful to give names to the people who employ

these skills. We find that there are four key players in meetings: **contributor**; **controller**; **completer**; **spoiler**;

Here is how each relates to the interactionist table; what the main skills are that each uses; and how specific responsibilities within meetings and committees, such as that of the chair, fit into this scheme.

The Contributor

The contributor **gives suggestions**; **gives information**; **shows solidarity**; **releases tension**.

The contributor is the person who oils the wheels of executive decision-making, and is comfortable in knowing that easing things forward is invaluable because otherwise things get sticky or creak. The contributor has his eye on the ball and passes it appropriately.

The secretary to a committee or meeting is often a good contributor. More knowledgeable of the past than other members, more conversant with the detail of the agenda and the papers which have been prepared, the secretary often facilitates in every possible way.

As with the other roles, however, that of contributor is not limited to one person. Being a contributor is the primary meeting skill: without contribution and without eliciting contribution from others nothing can happen.

A key element in contributing is the preparation for a meeting. In making it clear (rule 4: chapter 6) that everyone attending has an obligation to prepare, everyone is made to carry something of the contributor function.

Preparation has two elements in it. In rule 4 we stressed personal, prior preparation, but that carries over into the circumstances of the meeting too. If it's a golden rule of committees and meetings that by facilitating others' contributions you make things easier for yourself, the good contributor involves himself/herself actively at the meeting – provided always that s/he has something useful and valid to contribute – and eases the involvement of others. This may even involve making sure the layout of the meeting room is right, in the way a good crew member makes sure that ropes are properly coiled or stored ready for instant use. A poorly-arranged table – narrow and long when it might as easily be rearranged into a square – can make a meeting feel like twice the effort it need be.

By no means all the interaction at meetings is in the form of words. Non-verbal communication – reading the signs and signals that people send out quite unconsciously – will tell you what is happening and improve your contribution. Even when nothing seems to be happening, something is. Water without a ripple is calm and can be treated in ways that stormy water can't. So with meetings. If things are calm it may be possible to push on more rapidly and take advantage of the goodwill around. However, often at a calm meeting the chair relaxes and procedure gets sloppy, which is a very good way of bringing irritations to the surface. But clearly a calm and non-contentious meeting can be handled quite differently from one which promises to be full of conflict.

Peter Honey says that one of the characteristics of a successful meeting is that people contribute in an open, honest and enthusiastic way. If you have nothing to contribute, it's still possible to be open, enthusiastic and honest about saying, clearly and simply: 'Nothing useful to add that hasn't been said already.' Such a comment helps to keep the pace of the meeting from flagging.

Another characteristic which he notices is that when a group is skilful at meetings it can appear very informal. A skilful group can rely on one another to cope with whatever comes along. The chair becomes less controlling and everyone has a sense of responsibility for and participation in the outcome. Such relaxed meetings come, Honey suggests, from settings where there have been sufficiently challenging tasks to tackle; a reasonably constant core of members; and a meeting frequency of about once a week.

Fletcher believes that enthusiasm at meetings is something of which there cannot be too much. There is, of course, the irritating enthusiast, but such a person should be easily recognized as being well into her or his personal agenda, and so at risk of attracting the opposition that comes from self-display. Enthusiasm is not to be confused with the capacity simply to talk, nor must the enthusiast become too dominant. But enthusiasm is more likely to be a virtue at meetings than a vice – quite unlike when the established church was troubled in the late eighteenth century by free-thinkers and non-conformists, enthusiasts for their personal religion. A peal of bells erected at the time had engraved upon its largest member: Glory to God in the highest and damnation to all enthusiasts.

One method of getting enthusiasm up and running is to try brainstorming. However well prepared for a meeting, many people arrive hot-foot from some other activity. A little limbering up is no bad thing, in the way an athlete high-steps across the track and shakes his arms about before getting into the starting-blocks. The nonsense question we suggested before – how many uses can you think of for a hard-boiled egg? – is worth a couple of minutes of people's time and lets them change mental gear in preparation for the task ahead. Popular once as a device for executive training, brainstorming is now seen not so much as a way of getting anywhere serious but as a means of freeing communication barriers. But it does have its rules, and here they are:

1. Once the leader has given the focus for brainstorming, anything that comes to mind can be said, no matter how strange-sounding;

2. No criticism from anyone;

3. No evaluation of the ideas (that comes later if you want to brainstorm beyond the limbering up phase);

4. It's the quantity, not the quality, of ideas that counts;

5. Someone simply records what is said and doesn't brainstorm;

6. There is a strict time limit;

7. If used for limbering up, there is no subsequent comment about what anyone said (unless of course, someone saw how a hard-boiled egg could be used to solve the main agenda problem!)

Fletcher, ever delightfully cynical about meetings in all their aspects, says in his ninth Law of Meetings: *the only rule you need to remember about brainstorming sessions is to avoid them*. But then, he didn't think of using them just for limbering up. Brainstorming does turn everyone, even for a brief time, into a contributor. It also gets the creative, intuitive, rule-free side of our brains working, which is an important supplement to the logical, analytical side.

The place of briefings needs special mention. In the attempt to set up the volunteer service for alcoholics, what was noticeably lacking was a briefing to those participating. A major contributory role is to take the time and effort to brief people, and it can be turned into useful lobbying if there is something special you want to get through.

The Controller

The second character crucial to a meeting's success is the controller. Although at first sight it might seem that a controller should naturally be in the chair, this is by no means necessarily the case and often quite disastrous, though controllers often like to think of themselves as good in the chair.

Referring back to the diagram at the beginning of this chapter (p. 64), the controller typically **gives opinions**; **gives information**; **seeks information**; **shows antagonism**; **creates tension**.

A small software company, led by a very sales-orientated entrepreneur, ran into financial control difficulties. As a short-term measure, a financial consultant was hired to sort out the financial systems and take control of the cash flow.

The financial consultant had himself been in general management after qualifying as an accountant, and early on saw the small company's potential. By nature he was a controller rather than a contributor, and quickly set out to dominate management meetings. His favourite device for doing so was to ask aggressively for operating information and then give his opinion on its financial implications for the company – opinions which the other members of the management team felt unable to contradict. His undoubted financial skills left him in a position of considerable power among a group who were very anxious about how they had let things slip financially. Had the financial consultant been a contributor, he would have helped them to see how to use the information he had at his disposal and would have supported them in redefining their management tasks and skills. As it was, he used his natural style to develop a power base in an attempt to take control of the company. Not being especially skilled in managing meetings other than sales encounters, and being already anxious about their liquidity position, the other members of the management team found themselves outmanoeuvred.

Temperamentally, controllers want to have things their own way, and go for their solutions. They are necessary in meetings because there has to be a drive and energy that focuses on conclusions and output. But they risk being destructive because their personal agendas get very closely identified with the public agendas, and vice versa, so that they have a tendency to steamroller solutions. A controller is an invaluable member of a meeting or committee when s/he has developed contributor and completer skills too, and can keep a right hand on the control throttle. An unskilled controller is a dangerous hijacker. In the chair s/he leaves others feeling de-skilled and unnecessary. As a member of the meeting, s/he can appear to be fighting with the chair for authority over the meeting and its objectives.

A controller does not like brainstorming, because it implies loosening up and risking being out of control, even for a short period of time. In the antagonistic mode, s/he can look like a spoiler, but is saved by being a source of information and opinions as well as facilitating others in giving information.

A controller can generally be readily recognized by non-verbal mannerisms. By the same token, learning to adopt these mannerisms will allow you to function as a controller if it is not your natural style. Pre-eminently the controller conveys a sense of natural authority; looks directly at people and holds the gaze; looks over the top of spectacles or uses them expressively; sits forward to speak and leans back to listen; makes deliberate, slow stroking gestures of the chin, bridge of the nose or back of neck. Pointing a finger directly at someone, thumping the table, or getting up and walking around while speaking would obviously all be experienced by others as forms of control and attempts to dominate.

The controller especially enjoys an adversarial environment because it enhances the personal benefits of winning. (No good player of anything enjoys playing against a weak opponent. If s/he says s/he does, suspect something radically wrong or a personal agenda in full flight). Professor Joe Kelly characterizes executive meetings as ones in which naked conflict is likely to emerge, and in such a situation a controller is likely to thrive, honing his skills against those of competitors. It is very difficult for a new person to get into the workings of such a meeting as all kinds of private rules, statements and strategies have been worked out by the contestants, which the new participant has to learn. Such meetings develop their own rules for functioning in the context of the organizational culture of which they are a part, and require very strong chairing skills to make them productive and lift them beyond personal point-scoring. In such a setting contributors feel lost.

Another quality of controllers is that they believe conflict accelerates problem solving. This is simply a way of giving themselves permission to set up conflict situations – of rationalizing belief for their own preferred style, justifying it as a general principle which is not found to be true when closely inspected. Unfortunately controllers, being controllers, get away with statements like that, which leave them in control! These are the ace hijackers of meetings. Either the statements s/he makes are readily accepted, in which case s/he wins; or they are challenged, in which case s/he has created the situation s/he prefers and in which s/he is likely to win. It needs a skilled contributor to deal with this situation, who will be able to cast doubts while involving other people in such a way that the controller is not offered a fight. The goal posts simply get shifted. Even the strongest controller can get baffled under those conditions. As Fletcher so elegantly sums it up in his Tenth Law: *Even the world's most Machiavellian meeting manipulator can be outplayed, outclassed and outmanoevred by a greenhorn with genius and a smile.*

That, he says, is what makes meetings such fun.

Be that as it may, the natural controller does risk destroying meetings by shooting for (personal) solutions too soon. In learning some of the contributor's skills, s/he might learn to value disagreement emanating from others, and set out to understand what they are saying and where it's coming from, valuing especially the devil's advocate function (which is an extremely efficient way for a contributor to disagree without setting up conflict); encouraging diverse views; trying to offer ideas and suggestions instead of evaluating them all the time (to see if they fit in with personal solutions); seeking opinions and suggestions (the completer's special functions); and – most daringly of all – risking a look at group process.

This is an idea to which we have not thus far given a great deal of attention, but it is particularly important in the process of unblocking meetings which are getting nowhere. The essence of inspecting group process is to look not only at what an issue is but how it is being dealt with. The focus of discussion shifts, therefore, to 'how we are functioning' not 'where we are trying to get to'.

A good contributor will have no difficulty with this. A good completer will value its usefulness. A controller who has no skills other than control will be upset by it, and will try to put down the suggestion, classifying it as a waste of time – another broad generalization which, being interpreted, means 'it will delay me getting my own way.'

The fact is that all the time in any meeting there is an underlying process at play, just as in a petrol engine providing power. When the petrol is mixed with air and exploded in a combustion chamber by a spark with the resulting gases let out through the exhaust valve into the manifold and so away through the silencer and exhaust, everything runs smoothly and there needs to be no inspection of the process. But when the engine misfires or behaves in any other awkward fashion, some skilled observation is called for of where the difficulty lies. Similarly with meeetings that get stuck. They need skilled observation. If there is a process consultant on hand – someone whose designated task is to look at what is happening and to give feedback on what is going on underneath the surface – if the consultant gets it right the meeting will quickly unjam itself. But in the absence of such a person the group may have to struggle to find the answer.

That answer will almost certainly reside in people's feelings. If people have been feeling steamrollered by a controller, and in consequence feel negative, and in consequence of that have stopped contributing but are blocking, out of irritation, any constructive movement forward, then somewhere inside themselves they will know that they're feeling steamrollered. It may take some minutes to discover the feeling and put words to it, and sometimes a brave person to say it, especially if the controller has dismissed the process observation as a waste of time. But if one person is feeling it, others are likely to be suffering similarly. It's a great relief to all when someone puts words to it; the result is that energy begins to flow again; people take care they don't get steamrollered again; and, typically, the controller has to back off the solution s/he was after.

A good chair may get the meeting to look at process by adapting the freeze-frame technique, which is a training device for trying to look at what is happening while not losing track of where the meeting has got to. The chair says something like: 'Look, I don't think we're getting very far. Everybody remember where we're up to, but let's spend the next few minutes of the agenda finding out what's causing the jam. What's actually happening at the moment?'

A less elegant way of doing this is to call for a break. Moving around, letting people speak privately, exchanging thoughts during a visit to the loo, may often get the unblocking process going. But this usually takes longer, is more chancy, and doesn't necessarily involve the whole group.

A particularly pernicious process which needs careful watching and understanding is what has been called 'groupthink' (Janis). In groupthink, as Van Bergen of the Kellogg Company and Kirk of the Army Research Institute have described, too many heads spoil the decision. They quote Nietzsche's observation that madness is the exception in individuals but the rule in groups. Which correlates with modern social psychology findings indicating that groups are prone to take riskier decisions than individuals.

The special circumstances that create groupthink are where a strong corporate or other culture stresses unanimity; there is unwillingness to explore ideas constructively in the belief that exploration will be taken personally as criticism; and where any opposition is seen as inept or incompetent. These are circumstances in which the controller flourishes. The energies of the participants are over-focused and blinkered by a variety of subtle pressures. The belief that the group's actions have particular moral or ethical virtues can also be a powerful source of groupthink. It is tempting, and perhaps right, to ascribe Richard Nixon's downfall to this phenomenon.

So much for the controller. The central image to hang on to is not that s/he's the bad guy while the contributor is the good guy, but that the controller's energies are directed towards solving problems and taking action. In any commercial activity such individuals are likely to dominate, but they often do not use meetings well. They may get their own way, but there are other less expensive devices for doing that. If a meeting is about using all the energy available in the most efficient manner possible, controllers especially need to learn contributor and completer skills.

The Completer

The completer is the person who pulls it all together, and is typically good in the chair. The completer knows, intuitively, from experience and by the exercise of skill that committees and meetings of all kinds harness people's energies; that solutions will be found more quickly by using those energies than trying to block them; and that action will be more rather than less likely from such a process.

The special aspects of the completer are **expressing agreement**; **making suggestions**; **giving opinions**; **seeking information**; **seeking opinions**; **seeking suggestions**.

The completer is rather like a craftsman who looks at an object from a number of angles, in contrast to the controller who only wants to know what it can do. The completer values subtlety, diversity and difference, yet has a drive towards closure and completion which encompasses these complexities rather than denying them.

Completers know that decisions *will* come and solutions *will* be found, though not necessarily on a particular occasion. They are happy to decide not to make a decision when that is the right course of action, as they will know from the temperature of the meeting that any decision in such a context would be inappropriately forced. Completers are a mix of the reflective and the action person. The contributor tends to be reflective. The controller is a doer and concerned for action. The completer combines these qualities.

There is a kind of completer who is a worrier for detail and seems to be busy with the minutiae of what is happening. This is not a completer in the sense defined here, more a contributor: a person who wants everything properly tidied up. S/he can often be a good if pedantic secretary to a committee, but in an overall sense may not see the wood for wanting the trees to be growing in straight lines. The true completer not only sees the wood and its lie on the land, but can name the trees in passing.

The role and function of the chair has the next chapter to itself, and is implicitly about completers, so we will not dwell on them extensively here. However, there are perhaps two other completer characteristics deserving of note.

The first is that good completers are essentially free of hidden or personal agendas, in the sense that their personal agendas coincide to a remarkable degree with the public agendas of meetings – which is to engage the people there as productively as possible; to apply what controls are necessary to do so; and to find solutions which are from the common part of capabilities and knowledge present. Such a person strikes others as being essentially mature and comfortable within himself/herself.

The source of this comfort need not detain us. It can be acquired. For anyone who feels its lack, experimenting and risk-taking are required. These can come from membership of a meeting or committee. The skills of contributor, controller or (ill-advisedly) spoiler can also be tried out and incorporated into one's repertoire of effectiveness. The essence of the completer's capability is an essential regard for and trust in other people. By trust we do not mean blind trust – the kind of naïve person who often suffers consequently. What we mean by trust is that the completer has acquired the skill of valuing others' strengths, and believes they can be mobilized to the common good, while being usefully conscious of limitations and limits. The completer trusts his or her own judgement. Of course they will sometimes be wrong; from such circumstances are skills tested and refined.

The second particular quality of the completer is a thorough understanding of the procedure of meetings. There is nothing which diminishes anyone more than being unable to slip into the commonly-accepted rules of the particular encounter. The same would be true at a bridge table, a garden party, or in the queue checking in for a crowded flight. It is particular to British history and tradition that parliamentary procedures at their best have both shaped our national characteristics and are an expression of them. As the formal rules of committees and meetings derive directly from parliamentary procedure (as do the informal), it is a wise completer who makes sure s/he is not tripped up by not knowing the rules: just in case they're necessary.

The Spoiler

Alas, the spoiler can be found in too many meetings and committees. As the list of characteristics which follows demonstrates only too well, it's difficult to tell quite where the spoiler might be coming from.

Characteristics of the spoiler: **gives suggestions; gives opinions; gives information; seeks information; seeks opinions; seeks suggestions; shows aggression; creates tension; expresses disagreement**.

A particular difficulty with the spoiler lies not so much in the last three attributes as in the confusion s/he creates. The other members are essentially devoted to the meeting's goals and objectives, even if, as in the case of the controller, personal and public agendas are reckoned to be closely allied. The spoiler, however, is overbalanced in the private agenda, which permits both the free-ranging use of negative emotions which others, especially contributors, are likely to experience personally (the controller, as the basis for conflict), and the opportunity to come from any of the other positions except those which proffer positive emotions. The spoiler can offer positive emotions only in ways which are either barbed or sound/feel phoney with ulterior motives attached.

Yet, the diversity of human nature being what it is, the spoiler will be found often enough in meetings of all kinds. In work settings s/he may have some special skill which gives a credibility and licence to be tolerated at meetings or may, heaven forbid, have the power to be in the chair through ownership of the business or other cause. In less formal or voluntary settings, the spoiler's need to spoil makes his or her attendance at one meeting or another a forgone conclusion. Typically such a person is known as having a chip on the shoulder. It obtrudes inappropriately.

There are rare occasions when an otherwise responsible contributor, controller or completer may want to be a spoiler.

A woman being divorced unwillingly was in considerable conflict with her husband. Their respective lawyers had proposed a joint meeting to attempt a rational discussion of financial arrangements. The woman was convinced that her husband had stashed substantial joint assets away over the years, and had investigators trying to track them down. Her lawyer, however, was essentially a conciliator, disinclined to believe her and keen to get what he felt would be a reasonable settlement for his client.

She could not be seen to refuse the proffered meeting, nor delay it forever, but was quite certain that she was not ready, pending information she still awaited, to negotiate a settlement. Quite out of character, she decided to pursue the option of being a spoiler at the meeting. Adopting the position of being 'a difficult client' she interrupted continually, was arbitrarily capricious about saying 'yes' and 'no', and created an atmosphere in which no dialogue was possible. A week later she had obtained incontrovertible evidence of her husband's mendacity, changed her lawyer, and pursued her new action against her husband.

77

However, in the normal business of everyday life, the spoiler is a menace in meetings.

The essential question therefore is how contributors, controllers and completers manage to minimize the adverse effects the spoiler will otherwise cause. There are only two things to do. The first is to let the spoiler have first say, by the chair's invitation, so as to prevent him/her from controlling the meeting: it's very difficult for him/her to express strong negative emotions as the first speaker on a topic. The second is not to create conditions where the sabotage potential is made apparent to him or her. This is easier in structured organizations than in voluntary bodies. What is certain is that the presence of a spoiler severely diminishes the fun, though it does put a premium on skill.

Summary table

	Contributor	Controller	Completer	Spoiler
Shows solidarity	*			
Releases tension	*			
Expresses agreement			*	
Gives suggestions	*		*	*
opinions		*	*	*
information	*	*		*
Seeks information		*	*	*
opinions			*	*
suggestions			*	*
Shows antagonism		*		*
Creates tension	*			*
Expresses disagreement				*

8. The special skills of the chair

Groups which are leaderless are groups of a very special kind. All kinds of interesting phenomena happen in them, including finding someone to be scapegoat. Usually a leaderless group will, one way or another, find someone to be its leader. Most people function more readily and more happily when they know the structure in which they are functioning – where the boundaries are and what the rules are.

It is the special task of the chairperson to be identified as the leader: to know the rules, and to set the boundaries.

In many circumstances this statement gets inverted, and reads: 'It is the special task of the leader to be identified as the chairperson.' Often, alas, with disastrous results. For though chairpeople are leaders (for the duration of the meeting anyway), leaders are not necessarily good chairpeople. That is one of the things you will have to suffer in meetings. If you do find yourself in such a situation, adopting contributor skills which are chairing skills in disguise may be the best you can do, though you may sound like a busybody if your interventions are not well timed. Interventions have to begin with: 'I wonder if . . .' or 'It might be useful . . .' and so on, as ways of nudging the chair forward. But given that there is someone in the chair, what are her/his special skills?

We identified the completer's characteristics as most likely to be those of an effective chair, but, before elaborating on them from this particular perspective, some background first.

Fletcher quotes a judgement of 1894 which states 'It is the duty of the chairman, and his function, to preserve order and to take care that the proceedings are conducted in a proper manner, and that the sense of the meeting is properly ascertained with regard to any question which is properly brought before the meeting.' That seems like a good starting point, though not only British procedure can be brought into the discussion but, as Maggie Puregger does in *Mr Chairman*, Hindu, Armenian and Roman practices too. Chairing is essentially the distilled wisdom of centuries for the conduct of human affairs.

Five hundred years before the birth of Christ the rules of Buddhist monks included '. . . the holding of full and frequent assemblies, which met . . . and carried out their business in concord'. These do not necessarily demand a chairman, of course. The Quakers have a style of meeting which enjoins silence until someone is minded to speak, and eventually a secretary to the Meeting (which is what a congregation of Quakers is called) summarizes what is taken to be the mind of the gathering. If no consensus is found, the matter waits for another occasion. This is a form of democracy in the absence of a hierarchy to which many organizations would find it difficult to aspire, and perhaps for many it would also be quite inappropriate. The essence of the point is, however, that forms of conducting human affairs which require the maintenance of order and reaching consensus decisions have been in existence for a very substantial period of time. The chair of the next meeting is part of this tradition.

The judgement of 1894 sums the matter up very elegantly, though. Exactly how does the chair **preserve order; take care that the meeting is properly conducted; ensure that the true sense of the meeting is ascertained**?

Preserving order

The chair has the ultimate authority; how it is used will depend upon the nature of the person. The ultimate sanction – to suspend the business of the meeting – is rarely used and would require a particularly aggravated set of circumstances. The essence of preserving order is ensuring that everyone is heard fairly; that no one is allowed to dominate the time available; and that if there are procedural rules they are deftly and clearly used. A chair not knowing the rules is like a skipper not being sure, in a narrow channel with another boat approaching, which has right of way or on which side they should pass. It can lead to a great deal of unnecessary confusion.

Preserving order can also be helped by having the facilities properly organized. Start on time; make sure the arrangements are as comfortable and convenient as possible; let people know if there are to be interruptions for tea or coffee; and try to ensure that no extraneous matters intrude. The person who brings a portable phone into a meeting is a menace, as is the need for people to be called out to take telephone calls. If these events may happen, the chair needs to take a firm line before the meeting as to what s/he expects in the conduct of the business.

In informal business meetings these kinds of interruptions are legion. If you can't control your boss's habits, you can control your own. Any meeting you convene can be surrounded by an appropriate sense of decorum. Your secretary is an invaluable ally in this. If there are matters that will have to be attended to elsewhere during the course of the meeting, let everyone know at the beginning, remark upon it as a regrettable exception, and apologize appropriately. By such means you will set the style for future meetings. It has been said that good meetings are run largely on the basis of good manners, and there may be a lot of truth in this.

In more formal meetings where there is a proper agenda and minutes are taken, it is always good practice to ensure that members address their remarks either through the chair or to the chair. It stops direct conversations. Any side conversations which start should be brought under control immediately, as disorder ensues if subsidiary conversations are tolerated. Simply waiting in silence for a private conversation to finish is a remarkably effective way of stopping the practice.

Apart from suspending the business of the meeting for a period of time if tempers have become especially frayed, the chair can 'name' a member who persists in unruly or disorderly conduct. This person is then obliged to leave the meeting. Such practices are inconceivable in commercial settings, but not by any means unknown in the political arena.

In meetings where there are well established rules, standing orders and valued procedures, the chair also keeps control by making rules from time to time, or interpreting the rules in a particular context. In such a formal setting there will also be means by which the chair's ruling or interpretation can be challenged. In less structured settings, it will usually be part of the tacit compliance which members give to the chair that s/he can state rules. If there is a spoiler around who objects, the chair has the recourse of calling a vote by a show of hands. It is wise to make it clear that such a vote is on the matter in question alone and is not a vote of confidence in the chair. If the chair is being capricious and creating a general sense of discontent, a motion from the meeting that the chair stand down for its duration will soon test the spirit of the meeting. But any chair who had got into such a position, unless put there by a planted faction, would have lost real control some time before.

Ensure that the meeting is properly conducted

In an organized body which has procedural rules, this is a relatively straightforward matter and depends entirely on the complexity of the rules and the chair's understanding of them. However, an infinite variety of daily meetings in all kinds of settings are not so organized. What then?

We have already observed that hierarchical leaders tend to take the chair whether they carry particular skills or not. It's a wise boss who can assign it to a subordinate, seeing the chair not as a position of power but as a setting where skills can be exercised or developed. A subordinate who starts a meeting on time even though a boss hasn't arrived is learning some important strengths about professionalism in the conduct of business affairs.

In informal settings, the rules tend to be those which the organization has developed for the internal conduct of its affairs or the style and practice of whichever boss is in control. The larger the organization the greater the formality, because at least once a year it is likely to have a shareholders' Annual General Meeting, whose structure and conduct are prescribed clearly by law. In smaller, private companies or large commercial partnerships, however, meetings can be extraordinarily unruly affairs, largely because of the power structures and struggles of those attending.

When organizations are buoyant, they can perhaps get away with shoddy business practice. However, when they find themselves under commercial pressures or there is internal conflict, the lack of a body of experience which can resolve difficulties and differences becomes a great source of weakness. Typically, in such settings bosses feel unsupported; complain they can't rely on their subordinates; and tend to isolate themselves. Subordinates, on the other hand, not having been schooled in collective discussions which tolerated dissent and found conclusions, complain of being shut out of the problems and not being able to make a contribution. This tends to result in commercial banditry within organizations. Small factions pursue their objectives in an undisciplined way.

If you should find yourself in an organization which is weak on the methodology of its meetings, you can only try to ensure that your own practices are as thorough as possible and, when opportunity presents itself, develop the idea of improving everyone's skills by training. If you find yourself in the position of chair, make the procedures no more formal than the organization can tolerate, but conduct them with courtesy and care for everyone's point of view. You will eventually win, and on the way maintain your sense of integrity.

Ensure that the true sense of the meeting is ascertained

As the role has been seen over the past hundred years or so, it suggests a neutral chair elevated above the strife and passion of the committee or meeting itself who, from a detached and lofty position, summarizes what is going on and finds the points of consensus.

In everyday life this is usually far from the case. Typically the person in the chair – and the more informal the setting the more this is true – is passionately concerned with the outcome and often wants the consensus to be his or her consensus rather than the meeting's. How are these apparently disparate circumstances to be reconciled?

In the first place the members will generally have a very clear view of the chair's position: whether it is the detached, patrician form or the passionate, concerned form. Meeting members are typically not fools. But whether the chair is one or the other, if the meeting is to be other than a waste of time for everyone (except the chair pursuing a private agenda), the golden rule is to recall that the chair's job is to ensure that what comes out of the meeting is what the members can collectively be encouraged into producing. The skill of the job is to do just that. Like the conductor at the beginning of a symphony or the skipper at the start of a passage, the chair probably has a good idea of where s/he wants to go but has to involve the energies of others to get there.

In doing so the chair has four key tasks:

1. *State items on the agenda*
The items on the agenda state the purpose of the meeting, and the chairperson takes initial control of each agenda item by introducing it to the group, usually taking the opportunity to elaborate on the issues. S/he then opens up the discussion to general debate by inviting views from other members of the meeting.

2. *Elicit views*

Meetings are primarily about communicating. So that decisions can be made fairly and in an awareness of all the facts, the chairperson has to elicit people's views (if they hold any). This may not be as simple in practice as it sounds in theory, because personal agendas and group politics can be tricky to manage.

Nevertheless, without delving into this covert side at this stage, the chairperson needs to be ready to encourage the person who is shy or overcome to share any views they may hold, as well as to discourage anyone who is hogging the stage. It is also important for the chairperson to have 'read' some of the non-verbal behaviour, as this can contribute to how successfully s/he manages the meeting. For example, a person may be quiet for a number of reasons: is it just shyness and needing encouragement to talk, or is s/he displaying what can be called non-verbal *negative* behaviour (sitting back in the chair, doodling on a page, looking out of the window, yawning, etc)? The chairperson's skill is to react appropriately to deal with the situation. In thinking about non-verbal negative behaviour, the chair will need to focus on what has brought on the silence; is the person angry about something/bored by the pace, or what? Reading the signals carefully can lead to everyone's view being elicited – positive and negative.

3. *Summarize views*

In summarizing everyone's views and the decisions arrived at, the chairperson once again has the focal role and must keep the meeting moving along on track and in the right direction. At this stage, the summary should restate conclusions, decisions or views so that everyone present has a clear overview of how the group stands on the various agenda items. Summarizing also serves to focus people's minds back to the agenda. Very often, as happens when issues are being discussed among a number of people with different viewpoints, they get sidetracked or are inclined to go off at tangents on matters which are important to them but not relevant to the agenda item. Summaries tend to bring people's minds back into focus, so that the meeting covers the agenda agreed in the time allowed.

4. *Specify conclusions and subsequent action*

The final specific task expected of the chair is in summing up objectives which have been achieved or not achieved, as well as mentioning any other issues which have emerged during the course of discussions which perhaps need placing on a future agenda. Any subsequent action which may have been decided or needs to be allocated should be mentioned by the chair at this point.

Everyone should leave the meeting with a clear sense of the tasks completed; the issues which need to be discussed at the next meeting; the action decided upon; who will carry out what tasks, and by what date; any agenda items which did not get covered, and when they will be dealt with.

These then are the special tasks of the chair. It is arguably the most fun place to be in a meeting.

9. Practising, gaining skill, and having fun

There are four simple rules to follow in finding out how to enjoy meetings. Like all rules, they require a certain amount of self-discipline, but there is rarely pleasure without some attendant pain, and skills demand very little effort once they have been acquired. Like swimming or riding a bike, even though you're not absolutely fit the basic skill is always to hand. As it happens, meetings are such a continual commonplace for most people that there will be little enough chance for your expertise to fall into disuse. Like the skills of everyday life – cooking, perhaps, or driving a car – there is consistent pleasure to be had from serendipity.

The rules, stated simply, are:

1. Know what the purpose is
2. Use skills for appropriate input
3. Leave with decisions clear and tasks defined
4. Record the outcome

Let's take these one by one.

1. *Know what the purpose is*
Everything we have said about the agenda is crucial here. For every meeting, however informal, that you have attended in the past few months without being clear what the purpose was or without sufficient time spent in preparation with a known agenda and papers before you, you have risked less enjoyment and less effectiveness than might otherwise have been the case. The five

key questions (see chapter 6) which involve adequate preparation underpin this rule. Like all good rules, it's obvious, but
like many, it's often ignored. It's only the waste of time and
frustration that let you know it might have been done differently
and better – with more skill. Only you can put in the effort to
make the discipline effective.

2. *Use skills for appropriate input*

As meetings from your earliest cry in the delivery room to final
farewells are the stuff of human existence, it's not surprising that
when people arrive at the adult stage of their lives and formal
meetings begin to take over, they have skills of one kind or
another already in place, acquired through everyday human
interaction. Certainly by a person's mid-twenties the mix of
personality, experience and social style lets one see the embry-
onic contributor, controller, completer, or spoiler. If at this quite
early stage (even preferably at school and university) formal
skills in understanding and managing meetings can be inculcated,
a great deal of time throughout subsequent adult life will be
saved and better utilized.

Despite the fact that different organizations develop differing
cultures which have an impact upon the way meetings appear
to work, the essence of what is going on in all meetings is what
we have described here. On the face of it, the differences
between a well-run board meeting in a successful company and
the political positioning of an inner-city neighbourhood committee might appear to be miles apart, but they're not. In both
cases people have got together to achieve whatever it is within
their philosophies to want to achieve. The human processes are
then engaged. With varying weights and particular emphases
you will see the contributor, controller, completer and spoiler
at work.

Given that particular styles are as much a function of personality allied to self-developed social skills as anything else, the
skills task is the one which requires honing. A good navigator
(contributor) needs at times to be a helmsman (controller), just

as a foredeck man (completer) needs to be able to know at least the rudiments of navigation if he is to be a really safe member of the crew.

Meeting skills all rely primarily on the use of words – the way statements are made, views expressed, proposals formulated, and decisions conveyed. But it is not only the words that are used but the timing of what is said that is so endlessly fascinating. The interaction between people is a constantly-flowing process, made different by each piece of input and unique for that reason. Knowing not only *how* to intervene but *when* is the art of enjoying meetings.

There are no formulae for this. Watch people you regard as skilful practitioners in a meeting. See how they act deliberately and precisely: not as they would in dinner-table conversation, but with a heightened sense of their skills and capabilities. Look also at people who jam meetings up. Within the framework of observation that this book gives you, work out why. What is it that is lacking, inappropriate, or badly timed? The right conclusion at the wrong time is as much a bar to the efficient progress of a meeting as a bad summing up which doesn't quite pull together what had been forming in people's minds. In the way that a conductor is both the motivator of the music and the agent of the skills harnessed by the baton, so all members of a committee or meeting carry the responsibility for drawing out what is in the other players as well as playing (participating) themselves, a bit like someone who conducts from the keyboard while being the soloist.

Apart from observing as models those who seem to you to be less or more effective at this meetings business, is there anything else you can do to develop skill? The obvious answer, of course, is to set up training workshops in your organization. Whatever time your organization spends in meetings – commercial, professional or voluntary – if you believe they could be done better, some planned training might be the answer.

But if you want to develop this skill primarily for yourself (and then be a first division footballer in a second division side, which will tend to lift the game of everyone if you are willing to use your skills broadly rather than hog the limelight and de-skill everyone else), the second aspect to study is what your feelings tell you about the *process* of the meeting. Imagine your feelings to be like a radar screen. If you can keep your feeling channels open and not decommissioned by the stresses of whatever is going on; and if, simultaneously, you can read your feelings and convey to yourself quickly, simply and accurately what they are telling you; you will have much the best guide as to what is *really* going on in the meeting.

Earlier on we referred to the thinking/feeling split in the human system. The basic aspect is the feeling system, so it is this which in the end guides our actions, decisions and interactions with one another, whatever the subsequent rationalizations might be. Whatever the intellectual energies brought to bear on an agenda item, what happens to that item only makes sense, finally, by reference to feelings.

In an ideal state of personal inner harmony, thoughts and feelings are consistent and coherent, and they lead to equally consistent action. But to arrive at such a state the interplay between thought and feeling is a continuous process of refining. In some senses that is exactly what meetings and committees are about – finding the consensus view which integrates the majority feeling into a coherent thought for consequent action. In formulating a decision, a chairman will often say: 'Perhaps I can just test the feeling of the meeting by putting it this way,' and then go on to see if he has got it right. But it's the feelings, not primarily the thought, which he is assessing.

In addition to taking due account of good and bad role models and feelings, the other aspect of skill development to which we have made earlier reference (chapter 6) is taking risks. Trying things out that don't, first time off, feel either fluent or easily said, as one tries aspects of another role, does require courage even in small amounts. Rather than saying 'I disagree . . .', for instance, try 'Let me be devil's advocate for a moment . . .' It gives a completely different set to the person with whom you are about to disagree, and opens up a debate for others. Gradually acquiring a stock of introductory phrases gives you the tools of the committee trade. If you are primarily a contributor, hearing yourself adopt the tone and style of the controller will be an interesting experience, and perhaps in the beginning accompanied by a surprising amount of anxiety.

So these are the three main aspects of developing your skills

- use role models
- trust your feelings
- take risks

3. *Leave with decisions clear and tasks defined*

It is worth checking after each item of discussion, be it a formal agenda or not, that you know what the outcome is and what action is to follow. Otherwise what is left is only implications, and one person's implied understanding is often very different from another's. 'But I thought you . . .' is often the riposte to unfulfilled expectations when decisions and actions have not been made explicit. No one carries the responsibility for remedying this state of affairs but you, though if everyone takes the same responsibility life becomes a lot easier. If only you do, life becomes a little easier and others *may* learn.

4. *Record the outcome*

Formal meetings have formal minutes as a rule, with someone charged to write them up and circulate them. Informal meetings rarely have anything, though some organizations do write up a file note which is circulated to those attending; but this is often for meetings of a semi-formal nature, such as client meetings in an advertising agency.

It is a very good practice and discipline to keep a day book in which you jot down, very briefly, the date, time, purpose(s) and outcome(s) of informal meetings. It is an extremely good way to remind you of what should be done and might otherwise become sins of omission; of giving you something to reflect on, as a jotted note can often spark further useful thoughts; and in the end of having a record of what you at least thought was happening. If for no other reason than the last, a day book is a good idea, but it's rather a defensive reason. The first reason will improve your efficiency: the second will improve your creative, lateral approach to everything you do.

Do it.

Have fun.

Appendix: Some books and reference material and our comments on them

British Institute of Management;
'Meetings: – Setting Objectives'

A photocopied document of about three dozen pages, with some useful case-study material if you want to develop your training ideas.

Deverall, C. S., *Successful Communication*. (G. Bell & Sons, London, 1973.) Hardback, 110 pages.

Aimed essentially at developing supervisory skills, with main sections about getting words on to paper coherently, it offers basic suggestions and ideas which can easily be overlooked. 'You may need to cultivate a satisfactory quality of voice – do you sound timid or self-conscious or affected? Tape recorders are readily available nowadays . . .' Easy to be superior about its being a bit dated, but it is sound in a schoolmasterish sort of way.

Fletcher, W., *Meetings, Meetings: How to manipulate them and make them more fun*. (Coronet, London, 1985.) Paperback, 186 pages.

An advertising man's distilled wisdom from many years of wasted meetings. More a collection of one-liners than a book: full of useful and (if they were attributed) actionable quotes. Not a man to meet in a darkened committee room.

Honey, P., *Improve Your People Skills*. (Institute of Personnel Management, London, 1988.) Paperback, 192 pages.

Good straightforward occupational/social psychology well applied.

Janner, G., *Janner on Meetings*. (Wildwood House Ltd., London, 1987.) Paperback, 176 pages.

Janner QC, MP, on Janner, supported in a foreword by the Speaker of the House of Commons. More about public meetings and addressing an audience than we have been concerned with, and clearly from one accomplished in the art. Fits our category of controller very well. 'The object of a meeting is to win. To do so without opposition is a pleasure. But to overcome the opponent or the enemy, that is the truer triumph.' So that's what MPs are really up to.

Klein, J., *Working with Groups: the social psychology of discussion and decision*. (Hutchinson University library, London, 1963.) Hardback and paperback, 232 pages.

An elegant, thoughtful, uncompromisingly academic study of what is going on between people: firmly propounding an interactionist point of view: a classic.

Locke, M., *How to Run Committees and Meetings: a guidebook to practical politics*. (Macmillan Press Ltd., London, 1980.) Hardback, 190 pages.

About committees and meetings based on formal procedure. Good, methodical, well-organized stuff.

Peel, M., *How to Make Meetings Work*. (Kogan Page Ltd., London, 1988.) Paperback, 208 pages.

On the staff of BIM following a career in industry. Starts off with the idea of meetings as a vision of Hell (not many people use the capital 'H' there nowadays: he must be serious) and concludes each chapter with a short list of 'thought-starters' as ways of reflecting on what you've just read. Covers conferences as well as meetings. Highly recommended.

Puregger, M., *Mr Chairman: a guide to meeting procedure, ceremonial procedure and forms of address*. (University of

Queensland Press, 4th edition, 1980.) Distributed by Prentice-Hall in the UK. Hardback, 178 pages.

Apparently the standard text on meeting procedure in Australia, and so perhaps especially concerned with correct forms of address. *Inviting the Governor's wife* is a skill you may or may not want to acquire, but it's good to see formal modes of address to priests of the Anglican Church as well as other denominations being thoroughly catalogued. There is an extremely interesting table which compares the procedures of differing bodies with the noted authorities' recommendations on the matter.

Rackham, N., Honey, P. and Colbert, M. J. *Developing Interactive Skills*. (Wellers Publishing, Northampton, 1971.) Hardback, 191 pages.

Not strictly about meetings and committees, but thought-provoking if you're going to set up some training in committee skills.

Seekings, D., *How to Organise Effective Conferences and Meetings*. (Kogan Page Ltd., London, 3rd edition, 1987.) Paperback, 226 pages.

More about making sure it all works well than the precise detail of the meeting itself: a sort of executive checklist. Invaluable for anyone organizing a largish meeting which has to work well.

Stratford, A., *The Committee Book*. (W. Foulsham & Co. Ltd., Slough, 1988.) Paperback, 144 pages.

Lots of short sections on lots of things. Delightfully didactic – we are reminded that honorary membership, ex officio, is pronounced eks off-fiss-ee-oh; that very thin-skinned people should not be over-persuaded into standing for office, 'for office always brings a degree of criticism'; and that inaudibility can be quite a menace. Aimed mostly at local volunteer groups: 'Many groups appoint a sick visitor' (presumably for the sick, not ill herself). We find ad hoc is pronounced add-hock. It's all unfair to a Great British Tradition. Somehow worthy.

This, L. E., *The Small Meeting Planner*. (Gulf Publishing Co., Houston, Texas, 2nd edition, 1979.) Hardback, 262 pages.

A heavier version of Seekings, though aimed more at the smaller meeting. It takes itself rather seriously and the style verges on the pompous. But good in the executive checklist framework. A useful section on 'Conducting meetings with other nationals'.

Wainwright, G. R., *Meetings and Committee Procedure*. (Teach Yourself Books, Hodder & Stoughton, London, 1987.) Paperback, 181 pages.

Good, sound, practical detail, with a final list of the formal terms that appear in committees (like eks off-fiss-ee-oh).

Ward, S., *A-Z of Meetings: How they work and how to run them*. (Pluto Press Ltd., London, 1985.) Paperback, 214 pages.

If watching the proceedings of a TUC conference live on television is fun for you, this is decidedly bedside reading. It is aimed especially at 'people who are active in various political groups (especially the Labour Party), action and campaigning groups, as well as all the other organizations in Britain that make up what is loosely defined as the left'. And very thorough it is too. A good appendix on 'Meetingspeak': 'with respect/with great respect/with very great respect – these all mean the opposite'. There's also a guide to etiquette: 'Formal meetings. Don't start knitting or sewing'.

The Association for Management Education and Development (AMED) is the only voluntary association of professionals in the UK whose work focuses exclusively on management training, education and organization development. Membership is open to anyone involved in this significant field of work. AMED's fast growth in recent years has created a lively membership of interested people in business, government, voluntary organizations, academic institutions and managerial consultancy.

The main aim of AMED is to promote high standards of management performance so that people in organizations and communities can work with greater effectiveness. Members are therefore encouraged to meet and collaborate to improve their own professional capabilities. Activities include evening and one-day meetings, and three- to four-day events held all over the UK and in Europe. These are designed to provide members with different developmental opportunities for the various stages of their careers. They also enable members to extend their knowledge and skills, to keep in touch with frontier thinking on management, and to exchange ideas and experience.

Free publications are sent to members. These include *MEAD (Management Education and Development)*, a journal which has three issues a year and contains articles on current management training and development; frequent focus papers on topical issues; and a monthy newsletter.

For Further information, contact:

AMED
Premier House
77 Oxford Street
London W1
01-439 1188